Table of Contents

FOREWORD

They had just gathered in the Chief's Office. He called the hasty meeting of department heads to disclose the settlement of the discrimination suit filed by a police officer who was fired during probation for failure to perform duties. The Chief explained to his management team that one of the settlement stipulations required a thorough rewriting of the department personnel manual to comply with a multiplicity of court-ordered recruitment, selection, training, and job performance policies.

The good news was that the city only had to pay a $200,000 monetary award. The bad news was that the hard work was about to begin.

Here is a dramatic scene sometimes played out in police departments across the country. In a 1983 study published by the Police Executive Research Forum (*The American Law Enforcement Chief Executive* by Donald C. Witham), law enforcement chief executives rated legal problems and issues as one of their top five training needs. Many will welcome, therefore, the appearance of the present volume, which deals with personnel issues whose resolution, unfortunately, often begins in front of the judicial bench.

Stephen D. Gladis has constructed an administrative anthology which combines under one cover police personnel management problems and responses of recent years. He has culled the pages of the *FBI Law Enforcement Bulletin* to produce a sourcebook for police administrators which deals with the special aspects of "people management" from recruitment to retirement. Cover-to-cover reading gives one a complete review of current trends and recent changes in personnel philosophy and practice. Selective reading gives one a narrow but focused look on a specific personnel topic along with authors' bibliographic leads for additional study.

Police Personnel provides administrators with information and ideas that can help them meet the challenge of today's personnel environment.

Special Agent, Hillary M. Robinette
FBI Academy, Quantico, Virginia

PREFACE

When costs rise and revenues decrease, public organizations in general, and law enforcement agencies in particular, must find solutions to reconcile the dilemma of doing more with less. Because personnel costs for departments account for such a large percentage of police budgets, solutions to budgetary constraints should logically be sought in this area. Thus, the focus of this book: Personnel.

Over the years the *FBI Law Enforcement Bulletin* has served the law enforcement community well by providing a forum for sharing professional ideas and solutions. Recognizing the importance of personnel matters, *Bulletin* editors have focused on personnel as one of several major areas of concern and discussion. This book pulls together for the first time the most significant personnel-related articles from the *FBI Law Enforcement Bulletin* over the recent years into a single volume. The book compiles the articles, progressively, from recruiting personnel to training and developing them, to evaluating them, and finally to counseling them.

In the Introduction, an overview article entitled "Facing Increasing Crime with Decreasing Resources," sets up the premise for this book—doing more with less by effectively employing personnel resources.

The readings are then divided into four chapters.

Chapter I, **RECRUITING**, explains the recruitment process—getting the best personnel for the job at hand. "Law Enforcement Recruiting: Strategies for the 1980's," outlines the FBI's National Recruiting Program, which may provide a viable strategy for other law enforcement agencies. "Coordination and Consolidation of the Police Personnel Selection Process," provides an innovative, collaborative approach that can reduce the expense of recruiting. "Using Psychological Consultants in Screening Police Applicants," explains how the use of a properly selected psychologist in the recruiting process can save departments enormous personnel costs and, thus, financial losses down the line. "'Psychological Preparation' of Female Police Recruits," shows how, through a sys-

tematic method, departments can solve the expensive problem of female recruits who drop out.

Chapter 2, **TRAINING AND DEVELOPMENT**, looks at what you should do with personnel after you have recruited them. "The Training Director," discusses the duties of the training director from administrator to trainer, and from consultant to researcher. "Beyond Minimum Standards: Staff Development for Small Police Departments," argues that training and development must be a departmental priority and offers some realistic training suggestions. "The Stress of Police Promotion," describes the often overlooked stresses attendant to promotions and tells how that stress can be reduced. "Training Firstline Police Supervisors: A New Approach," presents a model curriculum for effectively training firstline supervisors.

Chapter 3, **EVALUATING**, examines the next logical step after training—evaluating personnel. Truly, both people and programs must be evaluated to produce an effective and efficient department. "The Performance Appraisal Interview," offers supervisors five basic questions to use in evaluation interviews and provides many other appraisal strategies. "The Police Problem Employee," describes "burnouts" and proposes ways to turn them around. "Evaluation: A Tool for Management," provides a description of the FBI's evaluation process and offers concrete suggestions about how to develop the same process in other departments.

Chapter 4, **COUNSELING**, details methods by which employees can give and get good advice. "The Employee Council," illustrates how a cross-departmental council can improve interdepartmental communication. "Peer Counseling: An Employee Assistance Program," describes how the Los Angeles Police Department's Peer Counseling Program has positively affected the department's morale. "High-Risk Lifestyle: The Police Family," describes the pressures of police work on the family and outlines why maintaining a balance between personal and professional lives produces a healthier, more productive officer. "Retirement: Is It the End or the Beginning?" offers the Cincinnati Police Department's preretirement training program as a model for other departments to focus on what is truly one of law enforcement's most neglected training areas: retirement. Finally, "Police and Personnel—A Continuum," provides the capstone for this volume and looks at personnel and policing of yesterday, today, and tomorrow.

Police Personnel admittedly has a limited scope. However, personnel issues have become ever-increasingly more important to the police administrator, and tightening budget trends clearly signal that personnel concerns will continue. Perhaps, if successful, this book will stimulate law enforcement professionals to focus on personnel issues and to share their innovative ideas and solutions.

Stephen D. Gladis
Special Agent

PART ONE

READINGS

AN INTRODUCTION TO THE PROBLEM:
Doing More With Less

"Do more with less." We in law enforcement hear this response especially when money is tight. No department has been more affected by tight money than the Los Angeles Police Department with Proposition 13 and its ramifications. In this article, Clyde L. Cronkhite frames the problems that face all of us in law enforcement, and provides some insights into equipment and information innovations that can help police departments do more with less.

1. Facing Increasing Crime with Decreasing Resources
By Clyde L. Cronkhite

Facing Increasing Crime With Decreasing Resources

By Clyde L. Cronkhite

Combating increasing crime with static or decreasing resources is a challenge for today's police administrators. This challenge requires us not only to work harder but also to work smarter to reach our mutual goal of providing a safe and comparatively crime-free environment for the public we serve. We can more effectively meet this challenge by sharing our experience—by sharing information about what works and what does not.

In California, we have experienced a substantial reduction in tax revenue due to Proposition 13, which was approved by our voters in 1978. This proposition limits property tax to 1 percent of market value. The results for the Los Angeles Police Department (LAPD) has been the loss of approximately 1,000 civilian and sworn personnel, a 10-percent reduction in our department's personnel strength. Because of this, we have been forced to manage with less, to experiment, and to research what other agencies have found successful.

POLICE RESOURCES

In the broadest terms, our resources as police managers are personnel, equipment, and information.

Personnel is, of course, our largest and most important resource in meeting the crime threat. Because personnel constitutes 80–95 percent of our budgets, when budget cuts occur, they usually result in personnel reductions. However, there are methods by which remaining personnel resources can be stretched to take up the gap.

Team Policing

In the 1970's, LAPD, as well as many other police agencies, adopted team policing, which was effective in reducing crime. While crime was rising nationwide, LAPD was able to stabilize and reduce major crime from 1971 through 1977, the years the department was organized around team policing.

However, with the loss of over 10 percent of our personnel in the last 5 years, it has been determined that the department can no longer afford this concept. Combining patrol, detective, and traffic functions into geographical teams resulted in administrative overhead and inflexibility of personnel assignments. Additionally, many of the community meetings that are fundamental to team policing were being conducted on an overtime basis and were paid from overtime funds that no longer exist. Even so, a minimum number of basic field units assigned to set geographic areas are still maintained.

Neighborhood watch meetings are held on an "as needed" basis with citizen volunteers so that officers are removed from field patrol for only a short period of time. The remainder of the field force is assigned where the workload determines they are needed.

Uniform Deployment Formula

To make the maximum use of available field officers, departments experiencing cutbacks are having to rely more on formulas that usually include calls for service, crime, traffic accidents, property loss, population, street miles, and population density. In the LAPD, a number of patrol officers are "reshuffled" every deployment period (28 days) according to this formula. Each geographic area is evaluated on the above factors and manpower deployed where the formula shows they are most needed.

Priority Management of Radio Calls

Several contemporary studies (particularly those of Kansas City, Mo., and Syracuse, N.Y.) indicated immediate response to all requests for service is not cost-effective. Consequently, a number of police agencies are now providing immediate response only to requests involving serious crimes in progress or where there is a present threat of death or serious injury. Other responses to calls for service are delayed and scheduled when sufficient radio units are available. In some cases, low priority requests are made on an appointment basis during nonpeak work hours.

In Los Angeles, under a program called System to Optimize Radio Car Manpower (STORM), a specifically deployed small percentage of radio units handle, on a scheduled basis, a large percentage of noncritical, low priority calls for service, e.g., barking dogs, loud radios, etc. Other radio units, therefore, remain available for immediate response to critical calls. Additionally, on all calls where a delay in dispatching occurs, a call-back is made to determine if the citizen still requests a police unit when one becomes available. This has reduced dispatching radio units when they are no longer needed. STORM provides the LAPD with the equivalent of approximately 56 officers in additional field time.

Some agencies, including the San Diego, Calif., Police Department (SDPD), have worked with their city council to establish a prioritized list of activities performed by radio units. By forming an agreement between the city council and the police department as to the desired activities to be performed, appropriate response times, how long each activity should take, and how much available patrol time should exist, they have established the basis for manpower requirements. If requests for service from the public increase, then the city council must provide funding for additional personnel or recognize that response time will increase and lower priority activities will not be handled. By this method, the council directly shares in the responsibility for proper service to the community.

Some agencies have strict control over the number of units responding to a dispatched call. Units other than those assigned are not allowed to respond. Additionally, units many not go "out to the station" unless approval is received from the dispatcher. To facilitate this procedure, field sergeants must announce their location by radio

periodically so nearby units can meet them for crime report approval in the field. Also, approval for booking is often given by telephone when jail facilities are located some distance from the approving watch commander.

Directed Patrol

Creation of additional patrol time alone does not ensure more police productivity. The Kansas City preventive patrol experiment called into question two widely accepted hypotheses about patrol: (1) that visible police presence prevents crime by deterring potential offenders, and (2) that the public fear of crime is diminished by such police presence. Many police departments, such as South Central, Conn., Kansas City, Mo., and Wilmington, Del., have found that to be productive, use of "free patrol time" must be directed rather than used reactively. They provide directed patrol by:

1) Identifying through crime analysis the places and times crimes are occurring and are likely to occur in the future;
2) Preparing written directions describing in detail the way problem areas are to be patrolled; and
3) Activating these patrol directions through watch commanders and field supervisors and assuring concentrated effort toward specific crime problems.

Expanded Use of One-Officer Radio Units

The San Diego Police Department conducted a comparative study of 22 one-officer and 22 two-officer units to determine the difference in terms of performance, efficiency, safety, and officer attitudes. Although the two-officer units cost 83 percent more to field than one-officer units, the study found that one-officer units performed as well and were substantially more effective. Additionally, the study reported that one-officer units had better safety records.

Motorcycle Response for Congested Areas

Response time to priority calls in congested areas can be enhanced by assigning motorcycle units to respond to nontraffic as well as traffic calls for service in congested areas during peak traffic hours. Because of their maneuverability in heavy traffic, they can respond faster than radio cars.

"Call A Cop First" Program

Studies have shown that many people call someone else (a friend, employer, spouse) before they notify the police of a crime. James Elliot, in his book *Interception Patrol*[1] found that in 70 percent of crime-related service calls, citizens waited 10 or more minutes before notifying the police.

Other studies (such as those conducted by the National Advisory Commission on Criminal Justice Standards and Goals) have determined the success of solving a crime is greatly increased if the police arrive within several minutes after the event, or better yet, while it's occurring. In response to these findings, a campaign to remind the public of the importance of "calling a cop first" can be productive. Radio, television, and billboard advertisements (sponsored by local businesses and the media), wherein the chief of police, mayor, or entertainment personalities make the appeal, can be instrumental in spreading the word. More productive use of officers' radio time can result.

Eliminate "Property Damage Only" Traffic Accident Investigations

Some police agencies have found it necessary to cease taking most "property damage only" traffic accident reports. This practice has saved the Los Angeles Police Department the equivalent of approximately 20 officers in field time. Units are only dispatched to the scene of such accidents to eliminate traffic hazards and verify that a correct exchange of information has been made between involved parties, but no reports are taken.

Increased Use of Search Dogs and Mounted Crowd Control

Besides using specially trained dogs for bomb and narcotics searches, these animals can be a great manpower saver when searching for suspects in large areas such as warehouses, department stores, and outdoor field searches. In a 2-month study of

LAPD's program, a team of dogs engaged in 165 searches, apprehended 54 suspects, and saved time equivalent to that of 11 officers per month.

Likewise, a few officers on horseback can provide crowd control equivalent to that of many officers on foot. LAPD has recently returned to the use of horses—something we learned from our Canadian colleagues many years ago.

Minimizing Report-taking Time

Many agencies are being forced to reevaluate their telephonic reporting procedure. It may be found that some agencies must limit their onscene investigation to those incidents where the suspect is still at the scene or very recently left, where recoverable evidence may be present, or where the nature of the crime or incident requires immediate response, e.g., violent or potentially violent crimes against persons and major traffic accidents. The San Diego Police Department now handles a monthly average of 45 percent of its calls for service telephonically with no adverse community feedback.

With cutbacks confronting many agencies, an evaluation of reporting requirements could be in order. Information required on reports that is "nice to know" may no longer be affordable and could be eliminated. Arrest, crime, evidence, and booking reports may have to be combined. The Los Angeles Police Department and Los Angeles County Sheriff's Department use a consolidated booking form packet which contains eight other reports, including a standardized front sheet for the arrest report. The information from the booking form is transferred by carbon paper to the other report forms. Also, some agencies are using "incident reports" to record only statistical information for minor crimes where little or no information is available that may lead to the apprehension of the suspect.

Followup time can be saved by allowing victims of theft-related crimes to list additional property taken (which was not included on the original crime report) on a separate report which is mailed to the police station. Use of this form eliminated the necessity of detectives having to complete followup investigation reports to list the additional items stolen.

Interagency Crime Task Force

Criminals do not often confine their activities to one jurisdiction. Combining investigative efforts with surrounding police agencies can often reduce duplication in investigations involving multi-occurrence crime trends.

Detective Case Assignments

Many police departments, including Rochester, N.Y., Long Beach, Calif., and Los Angeles, Calif., are having detective supervisors classify cases to allow detectives to focus their immediate efforts on the more serious, solvable cases. The procedure of the Los Angeles Police Department includes detective supervisors classifying and assigning cases as follows:

Category 1: *Require Followup Investigations*
Cases that have significant investigative leads and/or circum- stances which require a followup investigation. A followup investigative report is generally due within 10 working days.

Category 2: *Additional Investigation Required*
Cases that do not have significant leads initially but which, with additional investigation, may provide significant leads. A followup report is required within 30 days. If significant leads are discovered, the case is reclassified to category 1.

Category 3: *No Citizen Contact Required*
In cases that do not contain apparent leads in the initial report, detectives are expected to investigate when category 1 and 2 cases have been handled. These cases are reviewed by detectives and their supervisors to ensure knowledge of crime trends in their areas of responsibility. Detectives are not required to routinely contact category 3 victims.

Cases that involved in-custody arrestees are, of course, given top priority.

The positive impact of classifying cases is further complemented through the use of a form given victims by uniformed officers when crime reports are made. This form informs victims that a detective will not contact them unless additional information is required. This strategy thus tends to reduce the number of phone calls to detectives from curious victims only wishing to know how things are going on their case.

Detective Deployment Formula

A number of agencies have developed "work units" for the time it takes a detective to handle a crime, arrest, complaint, or petition filing. The average time to complete these work units varies and are established by periodic surveys. Detective staffing can be determined by calculating this information with the number of crimes in each geographic area and applying the percentage of work load in each area. Los Angeles, for example, uses this system to redeploy detectives semiannually.

Detective Complaint Officer

Significant timesaving may be achieved by having only one detective file cases with the prosecuting agency. This practice can eliminate wasted hours spent by detective personnel traveling to, and waiting for, available filing deputies. Other agencies have been fortunate enough to have district attorney and/or city attorney staff assigned to their police stations.

Another aid in the area of filing cases is to construct a filing manual that details what is required for successful prosecution for various types of cases. This can save investigative time often used to obtain additional information which the prosecutor found missing in police reports.

Oncall Court System

Significant officer time is expended in court waiting for cases to be heard. Many agencies have made arrangements with their local courts to have officers placed on call. This provides for more officers in the field and reduces overtime which often has to be paid back in the form of days off. Police personnel usually have to be assigned at court to coordinate notifying officers when they are needed. The return in manhours saved, however, is usually worth more than the manpower expended. LAPD, for example, estimates that their oncall system saves the equivalent of over 100 officers in field time annually.

Civilian Personnel

Most departments are expanding the replacement of sworn personnel with civilians, particularly in the areas of records, laboratory, traffic direction, jail, communications, property, supply, front desk, detective aide, and traffic reports. Persons trained to perform these auxiliary and support functions require less salary (and usually less pension benefits), and therefore, can provide savings that should be used to provide more field officers.

Manpower Supplements

Use of citizen volunteers, student workers, explorer scouts, and the like is even more important as personnel cutbacks occur. LAPD has created a reserve officer program that involves three types of reservists. First, there are the traditional reserve line officers who receive extensive training and are qualified to work in radio cars. There are also technical reserve officers who require less training and work the desk, community relations, investigative followup, and other such jobs. Specialist reserve officers are volunteers who have special talents useful to the department, such as chemists, technical writers, and computer system analysts, and are only required to receive several days of training.

Many departments are using volunteers to file reports, fill out telephonic crime reports (after officers determine what type of report should be taken), and conduct crime prevention training. LAPD has found that advertising in local newspapers is a successful method of recruiting volunteers.

As manpower continues to be reduced, some agencies are exploring the possibility of store security and campus police handling more police functions in their jurisdictions. This includes preliminary investigations, completion of appropriate reports, and the transportation of arrestees.

Increased Crime Prevention Efforts

A common tendency of police organizations in contending with budget cuts is to regard crime prevention personnel as nonessential. Thus, the reduction or elimination of a crime prevention staff is considered an appropriate economy measure. A more productive approach, however, may be to use these individuals as leverage in making the best use of available manpower. A few crime prevention personnel involved in an effective program can prevent crimes that would require the work of many officers.

In meeting today's management challenge, many police administrators are finding that economical crime prevention efforts are most effectively applied through programs involving volunteers. Under the direction and supervision of crime prevention officers, volunteers can:

1) Conduct crime prevention meetings in the selected target areas;
2) Conduct security surveys of residences in the target areas;
3) Distribute crime prevention literature in the target areas; and
4) Conduct an identification program that assists residents in marking their property for later identification if stolen and recovered.

Through these programs, a few officers can use the assistance of volunteers to amplify crime prevention efforts.

Even a large crime prevention staff can contact only a small percentage of the public. Television, radio, and the printed media, however, communicate daily with a very large segment of the population. By using the news media, a department can capitalize on the concept of manpower leverage (obtaining a comparatively large result through a process that amplifies the efforts of a small amount of manpower).

A recent U.S. Department of Justice National Crime Survey found that over half of the burglaries nationwide were committed against unlocked dwellings. If the public could be reminded of this fact through the news media, many crimes could be prevented. The chief of the Los Angeles Police Department, for example, recently made a number of 30-second videotaped messages on crime prevention. The videotapes show various crimes in progress. The chief is "chroma keyed" (superimposed) over the crime scene activity as he tells how these crimes can be prevented. These messages have been aired by many television stations in Los Angeles County.

Another idea is to obtain the services of motion picture, television, and sports celebrities in making television and radio crime prevention messages. Many well-known personalities are willing to volunteer their services. The idea is to make these public service messages "grab" the interest of the viewer or listener long enough to get the crime prevention message across.

The victim of a crime is likely to be more receptive to crime prevention suggestions than other persons. His or her experience as the victim causes the realization that "it can happen to me." The uniform police officer taking the crime report is usually the first law enforcement representative to contact the victim. This officer is in an ideal position to provide the victim with suggestions on how to prevent a recurrence of the crime. Field officers should be given special crime prevention training and handout material for these victim/officer contacts.

Crime prevention efforts can be greatly enhanced by the enactment of local ordinances that require "target hardening" construction in residential and business structures. It should be part of a police administrator's crime prevention program to encourage the enactment of this type of legislation.

Arrangements should be made for building permits to be reviewed by crime prevention personnel to ensure proper construction that will prevent crime. Another idea is to encourage insurance companies to give reduced rates on structures that have built-in crime prevention-type construction.

Task Force Organizations

As personnel reductions occur, there is a tendency to reduce planning and staff personnel in order to maximize the number of officers assigned to field duties. The resulting reduction of planning and administrative functions can cause great harm to the future of law enforcement. One apporach to this dilemma is to form a planning committee composed of all top managers. The planning entities are reduced to a minimum number of experts. As the planning committee determines needs for planning and other administrative research, task forces are appointed.

The task force members are selected from areas of the agency that have the experience needed for the particular task. They are assigned to the experts from the planning entities and return to their regular duties when the task is completed. This type of organization reduces the number of personnel permanently assigned to staff functions, yet provides for planning activities on an "as needed" basis.

EQUIPMENT

Reduced finances also cause a cutback in equipment, requiring judicious use of existing equipment. Additionally, the purchase of certain manpower-saving equipment may be cost-effective in coping with reduced personnel

Nonlethal Weapons

There is a growing need for effective nonlethal weapons because of the increase in violent mentally disturbed individuals and violent drug users. These persons do not respond usually to normal police restraints. Nonlethal weapons are needed to reduce the manpower required for incarceration of these persons. Additionally, they are needed to prevent officer injury which often reduces available manpower. Prime examples are the tazer gun and chemical irritants.

The tazer gun is now carried by all LAPD field supervisors. It shoots two barbs on electrical lines 15 feet, uses a low amperage, high voltage (50,000 volts at 7 amps) that pulsates at 28-30 pulses a minute and immediately totally incapacitates 80 percent of suspects. It causes no lasting effects, even on persons with pacemakers, and is usually effective on PCP suspects.

Chemical irritants are also carried by all LAPD field officers. They can be used up to 15 feet and cause vertigo, disorientation, and inability to act in 70 percent of cases. They have no lasting adverse effects, but may not be effective against persons under the influence of PCP.

Vehicle Deployment Formulas

Cost-effective deployment of automobiles, like the appropriate deployment of personnel, can be an effective "economizer" of existing equipment. The following vehicle formulas are based solely on personnel deployed and their vehicle requirements. The use of these formulas requires an honest look by management into vehicle needs vs. vehicle wants. For example, the factors in the formulas reflect different requirements for different assignments, ranging from officers who do not require a vehicle to officers requiring a vehicle 100 percent of the time. These types of formulas can ensure that personnel have vehicles readily available, thereby reducing down time or idle time waiting for transportation. (See figs. 1 and 2.)

Leasing vs. Buying Equipment

Some agencies are finding that funds are no longer available for the outright purchase of equipment and the building of police facilities. Leasing is often a way of avoiding the initial cash outlay and a means of surviving temporary cutbacks.

Hand-held Radios

Many police agencies, including Los Angeles, Calif., Seattle, Wash., and Chicago, Ill., have equipped their officers with out-of-car radios so that they are in constant contact. The cost of the radios has been more than compensated for by the added ability to call officers from nonpriority calls (such as report taking) to priority calls (such as robbery). As an alternative, some departments do not show their units "off the air" until they arrive at the scene rather than when the call is broadcast. This is accomplished by officers notifying the dispatcher when they have arrived and are exiting their vehicles.

INFORMATION

Alvin Toffler states in his newest book, *The Third Wave,*[2] that we are moving from an industrial society to a global society, which uses data to compensate for dwindling resources. Police administrators must capitalize on this trend and make use of information, particularly automated infor-

---

Figure 1

This formula is used by the LAPD to assign black-and-white radio cars to its 18 stations.

$V = .5 (n)(m)(d)(r)(a) + .5L.$

V = Number of vehicles required in the patrol fleet.

m = Maintenance factor (1.10) based on repair statistics.

d = Deployment factor (1.25) for variations in day-of-week deployment. This factor considers a 25-percent variation between weekends (heavy deployment) and weekdays (light deployment).

r = Standard relief factor (1.6).

a = Watch deployment factor (.45) for variations in number of personnel assigned to the heavy watch and light watch.

n = Total uniformed field forces including sergeants minus nonfield positions (desk, bail auditor, etc.).

L = Sergeants' cars on heavy watch.

Figure 2

This formula is used by LAPD to distribute plain vehicles.

$V = (N + .2F + .5G + 5T + .75P + R) - B M$

V = Total vehicles recommended for each entity by formula.

N = Personnel who do not need a vehicle, such as detective desk personnel.

F = Nonfield fixed-post personnel, such as staff workers. They receive one vehicle to five personnel.

G = Field fixed-post personnel, such as noncaseload-carrying detective supervisors. They receive one vehicle for every two personnel.

T = Personnel working two-man units on a full-time basis, such as narcotics and personnel investigators. One vehicle is provided for every two personnel.

P = Personnel carrying a full caseload, such as field detectives. The ratio is three vehicles to four personnel.

R = Personnel working one-man units and require a vehicle 100 percent of the time, such as narcotics investigators, supervisors.

B = Average number of pool vehicles used per day.

M = Maintenance factor of 1.05 as established by repair statistics.

mation, in meeting the challenge of the crime threat with less resources. We in law enforcement can make good use of automation in helping us to become more effective. Automated information can provide more rapid police response to citizen calls and faster access to information that assists uniformed officers to perform their jobs more effectively.

The Automated Want and Warrant System

In the past, officers have had to detain persons in "field situations" as long as 20 to 30 mintes while clerical personnel searched manual warrant files at the station house. Now it takes only seconds to determine if a person is wanted or a vehicle or other property is stolen. This rapid response comes through automated access to local, State, and national law enforcement files. This reduces inconvenience to innocent citizens and saves valuable field time for officers.

The Emergency Command Control Communications System

These computerized communications systems provide "instant cops" by:
1) Remote out-of-vehicle radios for every field officer that make officers available for response to citizen needs at all times;
2) Mobile digital terminals in patrol cars that provide field officers direct access to computerized information; and
3) Computer-aided dispatching of police units that provide faster police response to citizen calls for service.

The Electronic Sherlock Holmes

Two law enforcement systems are examples of how automation is used to communicate essential information and to reduce the time it takes detectives to conduct criminal investigations:
1) Automated Field Interview Systems—These systems link the thousands of daily observations made by field officers with crimes investigated by detectives. The computer connects suspects by location, description, vehicle, and activity to reported crimes.

2) Modus Operandi (MO) Correlation Systems— These computer programs process large volumes of data from crime and arrest reports and correlate incidents that may have been committed by the same suspect. By linking these reports through MO patterns, a conglomerate of information can often be compiled that provides valuable assistance in identifying crime perpetrators.

The Automated Police Manager

There are systems that assist police managers to use police personnel more effectively.
1) Automated Deployment of Available Manpower Programs—By computerizing information on calls-for-services from citizens, activity initiated by officers on patrol, and crime trends, these systems predict how many police cars should be assigned each area of the city by day-of-the-week and hour-of-the-day. They also give police managers information on the timeliness and effectiveness of patrol services in each neighborhood.
2) Computerized Traffic System—This system compares when and where traffic accidents are occurring and the causes with when and where officers are issuing traffic citations and for what violations. The comparisons are used to deploy traffic officers and evaluate their effectiveness.
3) Crime Statistics Systems—Through computer analyses of all crime and arrest reports, crime trends are reported weekly, monthly, quarterly, and yearly.
4) Training Management Systems—Officers' personal data, such as language skills, special occupational experiences, hobbies, physical fitness, training examinations, shooting proficiency scores, etc., are maintained in computer files so that training needs can be assessed and personnel talents and abilities can be properly used. Additionally, video communication is being extensively used in academy training and at daily training sessions. Computerized shooting simulators are also assisting in training officers when and where not to use firearms.

Microcomputer and Electronic Word Processors

Computers are following the trend of many mechanical and electronic devices that have proved to be helpful to mankind. Mass production is increasing their availability while decreasing their cost. Already the cost of minicomputers is within the financial reach of most police agencies. Today's minicomputers have the capabilities of larger computer systems of a decade ago.

Small law enforcement departments should consider purchasing minicomputers to supply most of their automation needs, and large police agencies should be evaluating minicomputers as replacements for their precinct station filing systems. In the near future, each commanding officer may be able to have a small computer for his use and the use of his personnel.

Word processing computer terminals should replace typewriters in most police agencies in the future as they are now doing in private industry. Crime reports should be "typed" on terminals. Computer systems can strip off information and send teletype messages, plus extract and transmit appropriate information for detectives, prosecutors, and the courts. Additionally, information for statistical and management purposes can automatically be transmitted to appropriate files. Much of the duplication that now occurs can be eliminated. After the information is once entered into the computer, the computer can take care of the manipulation of information that now is often done by many persons. These types of systems have already been put to use in some police agencies, but it will be some time before they are a common police tool.

Much of the processing time now consumed in the pyramid organization structures of police departments for correspondence, research projects, budget requests, and activity reports can be reduced by word processing systems. Currently, these documents are sent up the chain of command and returned for retyping when corrections or changes are desired by persons higher up in the organization. Often, they are completely retyped a number of times before they reach the chief of police. With a computerized word processing system, they can be entered on a terminal once and stored. When changes are necessary, the text is recalled on a terminal screen and only that portion to be changed is redone. When finally approved, the computer prints out a final report. Likewise, the text of routine correspondence can be kept in computer storage. When required, it can be called up on a terminal screen and appropriate names and text changes made to "personalize" the letter before being printed for signature.

THE FUTURE OF LAW ENFORCEMENT— SOMETHING TO LOOK FORWARD TO

When we talk about cutbacks, reduced resources, and managing with less, we often do so with a pessimistic air. We are going to have to deal with reduced resources for some years to come, but in the overall history of our societies, this will be but a short period. As we look back 10 to 15 years from now, we will probably reflect on this period as a period of reevaluation and refinement—refinements to meet economic and cultural changes. Review of our histories discloses many periods of reduction— a time for cleansing the systems, removing excess fat, firming up our objectives, and assuring that they meet the expectations of the public we serve. It is indeed a time of challenge, a challenge that we should look forward to with optimism, for the future holds for us an exciting opportunity to make constructive changes through legislation that can strengthen the judicial system and through innovative uses of our shrinking police resources. As professional law enforcement officers, we can help provide a safe environment where our citizens can exercise their individual freedoms with a minimum of disruption. And together, we can stem the rising crime with decreasing resources.

About the Author

Clyde Cronkhite is the Chief of Police of Santa Ana, California. He was formerly a corporate vice president for a leading financial institution and a Deputy Chief for LAPD where he had a 26-year career. He holds a master's degree in Public Administration from USC where he has more recently been pursuing a Ph.D. degree. He founded Forum 2000 (a future trends organization), has authored a text- book and published numerous articles as well as lectured, taught and consulted on police and management subjects.

Footnotes

[1] James Elliot, *Interception Patrol* (Springfield, Ill.: Charles C. Thomas, 1973).

[2] Alvin Toffler, *The Third Wave*, 2d ed. (New York City: Bantam Books, 1981).

CHAPTER I
RECRUITING

INTRODUCTION TO CHAPTER I:
Recruiting

The personnel process begins with recruiting. In order for departments to have excellent personnel, excellent recruiting is essential. This chapter focuses on several steps and strategies essential to good recruiting.

In some departments this is highly organized, in others not so. In Article 2, Kathleen McChesney discusses the FBI's National Recruiting Program in detail. This program may serve as a model to police departments to help them keep an eye on developing a systematized personnel recruiting program.

Article 3 addresses an issue close to any administrator: Costs. Excellent recruiting is a necessity, but it is an expensive process. Leonard Territo and Onnie K. Walker describe the cost-saving Police Applicant Screening Service system used by the Pinellas County, Florida, law enforcement community. This model—by using cooperation to overcome the ever-increasing costs of recruiting—may provide just the financial relief departments need.

In Article 4, Susan Saxe and Joseph Fabricatore explore the advantage of psychological screening of applicants. The authors contend that a psychological consultant who is familiar with law enforcement can save a department from the inordinate long-term expense of recruiting ill-suited applicants. They maintain that screening applicants through psychological tests, through in-depth clinical interviews, and through the background information supplied by the applicant, can effectively screen out potential liabilities for departments.

Article 5 addresses a serious problem for agencies intent on recruiting and retaining female officers. Authors Debra Furman Glaser and Susan Saxe note that misconceptions about the job and its impact on their lives contribute to attrition and need to be systematically addressed by departments to stop the trend of attrition. The authors present a viable model designed for the Los Angeles Police Department to combat attrition of female officers.

2. Law Enforcement Recruiting: Strategies for the 1980's
By Kathleen McChesney

3. Coordination and Consolidation of the Police Personnel Selection Process
By Leonard Territo and Onnie K. Walker

4. Using Psychological Consultants in Screening Police Applicants
By Susan Saxe and Joseph Fabricatore

5. "Psychological Preparation" of Female Police Recruits
By Debra Furman Glaser and Susan Saxe

LAW ENFORCEMENT RECRUITING: STRATEGIES FOR THE 1980'S

By Kathleen McChesney

The law enforcement community must locate and develop highly skilled human resources to face the challenges of crime control in the 21st century. Locating and developing this talent will be a difficult task, certain to be complicated by the competition between the public and private sectors for those same talented individuals.

In the 1960's and 1970's, national efforts directed at comprehensive crime control included changes in recruitment directions and strategies.[1] As law enforcement agencies began to seek candidates educated beyond the high school level, many State and local agencies found themselves competing against each other and the Federal agencies for college-educated candidates. Starting salaries for police officers in major metropolitan areas became competitive with their Federal counterparts, while some agencies paid premiums to employees with post high school or college educations in certain disciplines. Although the rate of law enforcement hiring is not increasing as rapidly as it was in the past decade, locating, recruiting, and retaining the best candidates remain critical issues for the law enforcement administrator. Hopefully, the applicant skills sought today will serve law enforcement's needs for the next 3 decades and the profession will continue to maintain a high employee retention rate.

Politics, socioeconomic factors, even weather, can influence crime patterns, and attempts to predict law enforcement's long term needs may be nothing more than projections of demographic data and statistics. In spite of this "best-guess" approach, a law enforcement agency that does not plan for the long and short term will need to retrain continually investigators with the skills (i.e., computers, foreign languages) necessary to address special crime problems. There are no simple formulas to assist the personnel planner in judging future needs; however, each must remain cognizant of ethnic and technical changes and how they may affect law enforcement in their communities.

A National Recruiting Program—The FBI Experience

The FBI's hiring needs are determined by several factors and are generally planned several years in advance of actual hiring. In the event of new investigative responsibilities or significant, unexpected crime problems, investigative personnel must be shifted in the short term to address the most pressing matters. Although the FBI receives thousands of applications for the Special Agent position each year, recruiting the most qualified candidates remains a serious consideration.[2]

In 1983, the FBI increased its Agent complement by 5.7 percent, and recruiters in the FBI's 59 field offices were advised to direct their efforts toward locating certain specialized candidates, particularly those with engineering, science or computer skills, or a foreign language ability. To unify, strengthen, and coordinate the 59 varied recruiting strategies which were ongoing in each of the FBI's field offices at the time, a National Applicant Recruiting Program was established. Included in the program was the development of a national recruiting strategy which would serve the FBI by assisting in identifying, processing, and hiring the best candidates for Special Agent and noninvestigatory positions.

Recruiters were tasked with matching the needs of the FBI and the occupational goals of potential candidates, a process which involves testing, screening, and formal and informal interviewing.

percent minorities and 39.2 percent women). Notwithstanding the directives of seeking specially skilled Agents, over one-half of the Special Agents were hired under the modified (now diversified) program, which requires a bachelor's degree and 3 years' professional work experience.[3]

Other law enforcement agencies, in varying degrees, can use strategies similar to those used in the National Recruiting Program consistent with the agency's or department's unique requirements, which may narrow the field of eligible candidates. The strategies described below, derived from past Bureau hiring practices as well as current personnel practices used in the public and private sectors, include: 1) the personnel forecast, 2) identifying an applicant pool, 3) needs matching, 4) intra/extra agency communications, and 5) process dynamics. Each component is part of an ongoing system in which the successes or problems of one component may directly affect another's function.

The Personnel Forecast

Forecasting is necessary when basic personnel planning is insufficient to predict future needs. Planners in the private sector have the luxury of current, valid market information with which to make strategic manpower decisions. The public sector, and law enforcement in particular, is subject to the most unpredictable events. Forecasting can be effective if careful attention is paid to obtaining sufficient, relevant data.

In many agencies and departments, identifying hiring needs occurs only at budget preparation time. Gathering information from all divisions relative to hiring needs should be part of a continual process, which includes the periodic redesign of organizational structures so as to provide the optimum balance between executive, manager, supervisor, investigator/patrol officer, and supporting positions (technical/clerical). Forecasting needs are to be expanded as far as possible, although some decrease in reliability is expected in multiyear periods.[4]

By seeking highly motivated, resourceful, and independent-thinking candidates, an agency will select individuals who will, in all likelihood, strive to improve employment status. In any pyramiding organizational structure, these individuals will, at some point, reach a plateau which they might not have attained had they sought employment with an organization where their highly valued skills and characteristics were not commonplace. The frustration which may result may lead to a retention problem.

Although the FBI, and law enforcement in general, has a low resignation rate,[5] retention is a potentially serious problem, particularly if those resigning possess similar valuable or unique skills. Ongoing retention studies are found to be particularly effective for large departments and should be conducted where possible. Apparent resignation patterns may be symptomatic of problems which are not obvious but perhaps easily resolved.

Identifying a Candidate Pool

Once it is determined what skills/qualifications are critical to meet personnel needs, potential applicant candidates can be identified and located. In addition, any special goals of the department or agency should be considered at this time (i.e., increase of certain minority groups).

Part of the National Recruiting Program's goals was to identify for local recruiters where potential candidates were likely to be located. Information was obtained from several sources—data compiled yearly by various public and private groups regarding college and university graduates, demographics, successful recruiters, and from an on-going survey of recently hired FBI Agents.

The FBI has always been fortunate to have a sufficient number of applicants for the Special Agent position; however, as the types of offenses and offenders have changed, many of the applicants have not necessarily met the current, more-specialized needs of the Bureau. As an example, the need for multilingual Agents has increased dramatically since 1982, while only a small percentage of new applicants speak a foreign language with the fluency necessary to conduct effective investigations. To deal with this dilemma, recruiters are directed to universities and colleges with strong foreign language programs or ethnic, multilingual communities.

Needs Matching

Current personnel systems are structured and modified by law, common practice and collective bargaining units, or labor unions. To be truly competitive for the skilled, college-educated man or woman in future decades, agencies and departments must offer more than a relatively secure career position and competitive salary. Today's applicants have social and personal, as well as economic, needs that they may seek to fill in the workplace.

The excitement and pride commensurate with a law enforcement career is often not satisfactory for a highly marketable candidate. Work conditions, organizational structure, ancillary services, opportunities for advancement, and recognition may be important employment factors overlooked in the recruitment process. When agencies desire the best candidates, they should be prepared to offer reasonable benefits and be cognizant of societal changes to modify working conditions to the new lifestyles. The agency or department which treats its employees as it did in the 1950's will not be competitive for today's men and women.

Intra/Extra Agency Communications

Through the National Recruiting Program, the FBI has been able to improve communication between personnel officials and field recruiters and between personnel officers and program managers. By promoting frequent dialogue between these groups, a framework for future effective personnel planning has been established. From the input (surveys) of recently hired Agents, recent communication methods can be reviewed and only those which are effective retained and/or modified.

In a media-saturated society, marketing is critical to hiring needs. Word of mouth, while extremely effective, is not sufficient for a total recruiting program involving substantial numbers of potential employees. Advertising is a critical recruiting strategy, and positive publicity should be encouraged. The National Recruiting Program has helped improve agency-applicant communications by using quasi-marketing strategies, i.e., up-to-date, full-color brochures and radio, television, and newspaper advertising.

Process Dynamics

Hiring employees is a process often regulated by law or policy; however, the process, as it sometimes does, should not become an impediment to hiring the best candidates. In a dynamic system, personnel administrators constantly monitor the process to insure that its structure does not discourage good candidates. Monitoring may be accomplished through statistical collection, interviews, or a letter card feedback system.

In 1982, before the National Recruiting Program began, the average FBI Special Agent candidate waited 22 months between his/her application date and date of hire. It must be understood that with fewer positions available than the number of candidates and externally imposed fluctuations in hiring levels, there will be some lag time between application and hiring. Due to the nature of employment, extensive and time-consuming background checks must be conducted.

One of the main priorities of the National Applicant Recruiting Program was to improve the hiring process in both quality and efficiency. Moreover, through the efforts of the Personnel Office, computerization of testing and test results was improved. A significant new program was established to train applicant interviewers and recruiters nationwide, coupled with an advertising campaign that revamped and revitalized dated recruitment material.

One segment of the National Recruiting Program involves an ongoing survey of recently hired Agents with regard to two factors: 1) the most positive or negative factors influencing their decision to seek a law enforcement career (in this case with the FBI) and 2) what recruiting strategies, techniques, or events, if any, influenced their decision to join the FBI.[6]

With regard to motivational factors, most recruits were found to have joined the FBI for several similar reasons. Those factors were professional image of the FBI, personal knowledge of FBI Agents, and national reputation of the FBI.

Similarly, the most important recruiting technique or event noted was a positive personal contact between the candidate and an individual who was a Special Agent. The importance of the role-model approach, heretofore assumed, is now quantified.

Instead of a limited number of field recruiters, there is a potential for the entire Special Agent population (over 8,000 Special Agents) to recruit new Agents. The FBI's recruiting survey can be adapted to all levels of law enforcement and is available through the FBI's Human Resource Planning Office.[7]

Intraagency communication is thus significant in making each Agent aware of his/her recruiting responsibility. Every contact Special Agents, investigators, or police officers make with law-abiding citizens is a potential recruiting contact. Important investigations resulting in positive publicity have the value of advertising the agency and its personnel. Likewise, negative publicity deters some good candidates who are affected by peer pressure or are unable to see beyond the criticism.

The National Recruiting Program has proven to be a successful method of recruiting on a large scale. Currently, the time elapsed for the average recruit between initial application and date of hire is 12 months. Test results are completed within 2 months, and within 4 months, individuals are advised if they are viable Special Agent candidates. The program was established with a built-in flexibility so that as personnel needs change directives are easily modified. Agency needs obviously vary; therefore, what benefits an agency of 20,000 may not work for a smaller or larger agency. Many of the basic concepts, however, (planning, communication, adaptability) can be tailored to any agency's personnel functions.

Minority Hiring—A Special Problem

The FBI seeks to recruit the most qualified men and women of all races. Demographic factors still affirm that there are fewer potential candidates in some categories based on smaller numbers of individuals having the prerequisite qualifications for the Special Agent position. Various groups of potential candidates are not equally drawn toward the law enforcement profession; however, those that are seem to be drawn for many of the same reasons.

For law enforcement agencies such as the FBI, where a college degree is required of all applicants, a look at the composition of graduating college classes indicates fewer minority (black) graduates in the near future.[8] With reduced numbers of blacks eligible to apply for some law enforcement jobs, and increased competition with the private sector for the minority employee, there may be profound difficulties in minority hiring in the 1990's.

Human Resource Planning

What can be done if attempts at human resource planning fall short of law enforcement needs? Law enforcement agencies need to employ continually a base of investigative generalists, complemented by specialists, and to update inservice training programs to insure that investigative abilities meet investigative needs. To fill an agency's current needs with only specialists will produce a glut of personnel who, during a crucial, changing period, may be unable to vary their investigative outlook.

The FBI's National Recruiting Program has developed into a human resources planning group designed to meet the rapidly changing demands of the Bureau's varied law enforcement responsibilities. Not all agencies or departments have the need for full-time personnel specialists, but all law enforcement agencies need someone who is responsible for human resource planning. Planning, combined with flexible personnel policies, will assist the public personnel administrator in meeting future needs with competent, motivated employees who will make significant contributions to the criminal justice system.

About the Author

Kathleen L. McChesney is a Special Agent of the Federal Bureau of Investigation (FBI) currently serving as a Supervisory Special Agent (SSA) at FBI Headquarters, Washington, D.C. Ms. McChesney has been an Instructor at Seattle University and the Washington State Police Academy. She possesses a Bachelor of Science Degree in Police Science and Administration from Washington State University, a Master of Arts in Public Administration from Seattle University, and a Ph.D. in Public Administration from Golden Gate University, San Francisco.

Footnotes

[1] National Advisory Commission on Criminal Justice Standards and Goals. *Police* (Washington, D.C.: U.S. Government Printing Office, 1973).

[2] The FBI tests (including retests) approximately 12,000 candidates per year. In 1982, 350 Special Agents were hired, 666 in 1983, and 672 in 1984.

[3] The FBI hires Special Agents under one of five program areas designed to meet the Bureau's diverse needs—law, accounting, science/engineering, diversified, and foreign language.

[4] Gary Dressler, *Personnel Management* (Reston, VA: Prentice-Hall, 1984), p. 113.

[5] Bureau of National Affairs, *Job Absence and Turnover* (Washington, D.C.: U.S. Government Printing Office, 1981, 1982, and 1983).

[6] O. Glenn Stahl, *Public Personnel Administration* (New York, NY: Harper and Row, 1983). "It is incumbent upon the personnel agency to test the success of its various recruitment policies by keeping a check on the results."

[7] Human Resource Planning Office, Federal Bureau of Investigation, J.E. Hoover Building, 9th & Pennsylvania Ave. NW, Washington, D.C. 20535.

[8] *The Washington Post*, "Black Enrollment in Colleges Found to be Declining Nationwide." 7/6/85. College eligible blacks going on to college decreased 11 percent between 1975 and 1981; however, the number of female college students continues to increase.

Coordination and Consolidation of the Police Personnel Selection Process

By Leonard Territo
and
Onnie K. Walker

An area of rapidly growing concern in law enforcement is the selection process for police officers. This concern is valid for at least two reasons. First, the ultimate success of any organization, regardless of its nature or purpose, is primarily dependent on the competence of its personnel. All other organizational resources are less valuable until personnel are properly selected and trained.

The selection process is especially critical as it applies to law enforcement agencies. Because a police officer is entrusted with awesome power and responsibility, administrators must take special care to insure that only highly capable individuals are permitted to serve. Failure to do so could have serious consequences for the law enforcement agency, the individual police officer, and the citizens.

A second major factor in the need for a careful personnel selection process is the necessity for guaranteeing that each applicant is processed in accordance with equal opportunity employment procedures.[1]

In an effort to accomplish these goals in an effective and economic manner, the chiefs of police in Pinellas County, Fla., and the county sheriff agreed in 1975 to work toward the coordination and consolidation of all phases of the police personnel selection process. Pinellas County has 20 municipal police departments and a single sheriff's department. The two largest cities in this south central county of Florida are St. Petersburg and Clearwater.

The decision to consider consolidating segments of this highly specialized police function was made for a number of reasons. First, it was considered to be more cost effective to have these functions performed by one group of highly trained and carefully selected individuals rather than to have them handled in a nonuniform way by officers from different police departments in Pinellas County. Second, the implementation of such a practice assured a high degree of quality control in all phases of the screening process—assurance that could not be given under the previous system.[2] Created to perform this function was the Police Applicant Screening Service (PASS) which was made a part of the Pinellas Standards Council.

The PASS team is comprised of four staff members: a supervisor, two investigators, and a polygraph examiner employed to perform this function exclusively. The PASS office also has two full-time secretaries.

Applicant Sign In

When individuals indicate an interest in being employed as a law enforcement officer in Pinellas County, they are requested to "sign in," at which time they are furnished a file jacket with their file number. The folder contains the following forms which the applicant is required to complete, sign, and date:

1) Equal employment opportunity questionnaire;
2) Police applicant screening service procedures;
3) Selection standards for police officer position in Pinellas County;
4) PASS policies;
5) Application for police screening;
6) Previous law enforcement background;
7) Waiver of damage claim by applicants;
8) Military Statement Form 180N, "requests pertaining to military records";
9) Educational letters;

10) Personal inquiry waiver authority for release of information; and
11) Liability waiver.

Written Test

Applicants are given one of three different tests comprised of 120 multiple-choice questions. All three examinations have essentially the same type of questions. An applicant must make a minimum score of 60 to pass. The test is graded in his presence at the PASS office. If he fails the first written test, he is informed at the time that he can take a second test that same day if he chooses, or he may return at a later date. If the applicant fails the second test, his file is administratively closed, and he will not be given an opportunity for further examinations.

When an applicant passes the written test, he is advised that the next phase of the process is the completion of the physical agility test. He is informed of the various segments of the test and is advised when and where the test will be conducted.

Agility Test

The physical agility test is given two times, one day a week. Applicants are immediately advised whether they have passed the test. If they fail, they may be retested at the next regularly scheduled time. There is no limit to the number of times an applicant may take this test.

Personal History Form

If an applicant passes the physical agility test, he is furnished a personal history form. Upon completion of this form, the applicant is scheduled for a polygraph interview. Failure to return the personal history form within 2 weeks will result in the applicant's file being administratively closed.

Polygraph Interview

The polygraph interview, conducted at the PASS office, takes approximately 2 to 3 hours to administer. Before the creation of PASS, there was no uniformity regarding the use of the polygraph in the preemployment screening process. In some in-

stances, Pinellas County police departments used their own departmental polygraph examiners for the screening process. In other cases, police departments chose not to use the polygraph, while still others employed private polygraph examiners. With the creation of PASS and the employment of a single highly qualified polygraph examiner, uniformity and quality control were assured. In addition, there are now standardized polygraph questions.

Once the polygraph examination is completed, the findings are forwarded to the advisory council, and the applicant is fingerprinted and photographed. The fingerprints are then forwarded to FBI Headquarters in Washington, D.C.

Review of Applicant's File

The advisory committee of the Pinellas County Police Standards Council meets once a month and reviews all applicant files to determine whether the PASS office should continue its screening process. If an applicant is deemed unacceptable, he is so informed. If the applicant is acceptable, notification is sent to him, advising him when to appear for an oral board interview. If it is determined that an applicant does not meet selection standards, he may appeal the advisory committee's decision by writing a letter to the chairman of the Pinellas County Police Standards Council who will arrange to reintroduce the applicant's case, along with the applicant's appeal comments, to the advisory committee. If the appeal is granted, the advisory committee will order PASS to continue processing the applicant.

Oral Board

The oral board, which meets once a month, usually consists of a member of the Pinellas Police Academy staff, two sergeants, and two patrol officers. Each police officer must be from a different Pinellas County police agency, and oral board members may vary each month. Board members are selected from a list of suitable personnel provided by each police department. All police officers on this list are volunteers who have at least 3 years of law enforcement experience.

Members of the oral board grade the applicants independently. If applicants are determined to be unacceptable—a passing score of 60 has been set—they are informed, in writing, by the PASS office.

If the applicant is deemed acceptable by the oral board, arrangements are made to schedule the applicant for a medical examination.

Background Investigation

The background investigation is expensive and time-consuming. Prior to PASS, there was usually not a particular individual within an agency specifically assigned to perform this function. The task might have been given to a detective who had other responsibilities or perhaps even to a patrol officer who was advised to conduct the background investigation when not on an assignment. This type of hit-and-miss approach to background investigations may result in the employment of officers who are not suited for police work.

Background investigations are, in every respect, as specialized as other types of police investigations, making it essential that the person responsible for conducting the investigation be both experienced and knowledgeable.

Completion of Investigation

When all phases of the preselection process are completed, applicant information is assembled in a permanent file which is placed in the candidates' pool. These applicants are available for review for prospective positions by members of the council or their authorized representatives.

If an applicant specifies a preference for a particular agency, a memo indicating agency preference is placed in his file. In some cases, an applicant is referred to the PASS office by a particular law enforcement agency; however, if the applicant is deemed acceptable, he is not obligated to go to work for the agency making the referral.

It is important to note that some Pinellas County law enforcement agencies impose additional steps to the preemployment screening process for those applicants they are interested in employing. For example, some agencies require their applicants to take psychological tests; others use their own oral board. This allows maximum freedom to be retained by the law enforcement agencies in the selection process.

Voluntary Participation

Law enforcement agencies in Pinellas County are not compelled to participate in the PASS program and may decide to take advantage of only a portion of the service. At this time, however, all agencies participate in PASS, either completely or quite extensively. Even if a law enforcement administrator decides not to participate, representatives from that department may still sit on the advisory council.

Funding

One of the many positive features of the PASS program is that it is free to the participating law enforcement agencies, taxpayers, and applicants. The entire program is funded from a $1 surcharge imposed on all traffic fines and misdemeanor offenses in Pinellas County. All monies emanating from this source are used exclusively for the financial needs of PASS.

Conclusion

The PASS program has considerable merit for those parts of the country which have many law enforcement agencies in a relatively close or contiguous geographic region. The concept works to the advantage of both the applicant and the participating law enforcement agencies.

The system is advantageous to the applicant because he no longer has to contact a large number of agencies to get information about entrance requirements, salaries, and availability of positions. Additionally, he does not have to take numerous entrance examinations, polygraph examinations, or oral board interviews required in the preemployment screening process.

There is general agreement that PASS is much more cost effective than having individual agencies complete their own selection process. In the past, each police agency had to absorb the total cost of the salaries of investigative personnel, staff support, clerical workers, office space, and all of the other administrative costs associated with the process. With the development of PASS, agencies can now consolidate and coordinate the police personnel selection process.

About the Authors

Dr. Leonard Territo is presently a Professor of Criminology, University of South Florida, Tampa, Florida. Prior to joining the faculty of the University of South Florida, he served first as a Major and then as Chief Deputy (Undersheriff) with the Leon County Sheriff's Department, Tallahassee, Florida. He also served for almost nine years with the Tampa Police Department. Dr. Territo is the former chairman of the Department of Police Administration and Director of the Florida Institute for Law Enforcement at St. Petersburg Junior College, St. Petersburg, Florida. His academic credentials include an Associate in Arts in Police Administration from St. Petersburg Junior College, a Bachelor of Arts in Interdisciplinary Social Sciences, and a Master of Arts in Political Science from the University of South Florida, and a Doctor of Education from Nova University.

He has coauthored some of the leading books in the law enforcement profession including: Police Administration, *which is in its second edition;* Criminal Investigation, *which is in its fourth edition;* Stress and Police Personnel; The Police Personnel Selection Process; Crime and Justice in America: A Human Perspective; Police Civil Liability, *and* Hospital and College Security Liability. *He has had numerous articles published in nationally recognized law enforcement and legal journals.*

Onnie Walker, a thirty year veteran of the FBI, entered on duty as an FBI Special Agent in September, 1947. His first office was Dallas, followed by Miami. In 1950, Onnie was stationed in the Tampa office where he remained until December, 1980, when he retired after thirty years of service. Following his retirement, Onnie went to work as a supervisor of the Police Applicant Screening Services on the Pinellas Police Standards Council in Clearwater, Florida. Onnie worked with the Council until March, 1982, when he became fully retired. He now enjoys golf and traveling. Onnie

and his wife have three adult daughters and live in Tampa, Florida.

Footnotes

[1] L. Territo, C.R. Swanson, Jr., and Neil C. Chamelin, *The Police Personnel Selection Process* (Indianapolis, Ind.: Bobbs-Merrill Educational Publishing, 1977), p. vii.

[2] Considerable differences were found in the background investigation practices of Pinellas County police departments in a study conducted by L. Territo. See L. Territo, *A Study of Police Personnel Character Investigation Practices of Municipal Departments in the State of Florida.* (Tampa, Fla.: Unpublished master's thesis, University of South Florida, Tampa, 1971).

Using Psychological Consultants in Screening Police Applicants

By Susan Saxe
and
Joseph Fabricatore

Since the Kerner Commission's recommendation in 1967 that all police officers be psychologically evaluated, psychological screening of applicants has become a routine component of the hiring process in many police agencies. Although the psychological evaluation process is widely used, it has not always been well understood or used to maximum effectiveness. Therefore, it is necessary to clarify some of the basic issues involved in effectively incorporating the "psychological" into the law enforcement administrative process.

Stress, "Liability-Prone," and Negligent Admission/Retention

Research shows that excessive stress can lead to aggressive and unconventional behavior, as well as mental and physical dysfunctions on the job.[1] Police work is a well-known, high-stress occupation. Stress can be a significant factor in causing serious and expensive problems, but the stress tolerance level of officers or applicants can be a significant factor in preventing problems. People have different ways of coping with stress. Some individuals are emotionally "liability-prone." These individuals have an increased propensity to develop serious behavioral, psychological, and physical problems. They may become a serious threat to themselves, fellow officers, the welfare of the community, and the agency budget.

Apart from the obvious moral obligation law enforcement agencies have to ensure that their officers do not abuse their powers, inappropriate police behavior is expensive. The cost of investigating and processing personnel complaints is high. Disciplinary actions often include suspension, which reduces manpower. In addition, lawsuits and civil claims are costly in both dollars and man-power and are devastating to agency morale. The courts have identified "negligent admission" and "negligent retention" of officers as agency liabilities. Most agencies can trace a major portion of their unfavorable incidents to a relatively small number of officers. It is in the area of identifying applicants whose behavior will be costly to the agency that psychological screening efforts can be most effective.

Strategies—"Select In" or "Screen Out"

Too often, police administrators are led to believe in a "select in" strategy, which suggests that psychological evaluations can aid in selecting the best candidate for police work. This is not quite true. Psychological inputs can be helpful in deciding which individuals within an agency or department are suitable for specific assignments, such as Special Weapons and Tactics (SWAT), hostage negotiation, or bomb squads, but the most effective use of psychological evaluation is to "screen out" or identify those applicants who may not be emotionally suitable or may be a high risk for law enforcement. In our experience, the percentage of applicants psychologically unsuitable typically ranges between 5 percent and 20 percent of the applicant pool.

The former strategy—"select in"—implies a precision and level of accuracy that psychologists do not possess and psychological procedures do not produce. In addition, this strategy ignores the possibility that future events, such as personal problems, could severely impact applicants initially judged to be acceptable and cause them to become high-risk employees at a later time.

Unsuitable applicants do not always appear to be inappropriate. Applicant pools approximate the normal curve—some individuals will appear to be excellent candidates, some will be obviously unacceptable, and the great majority will be somewhere in the middle. Applicants in this middle range who, in the judgment of a psychologist, demonstrate risk of engaging in liability-resulting behavior should be screened out. This decision is not always clear, but in admitting individuals to law enforcement, judgmental decision should be made with caution.

Other mechanisms should exist in the screening process to minimize possible decision errors. Included should be an appeal or review process conducted at a higher administrative level.

How to Select and Best Use a Psychological Consultant

It would be ideal for law enforcement agencies to have a full-time mental health professional as part of the staff. In this case, the professional should be involved in an orientation period long enough to provide familiarity with police management, police officers' tasks, and criteria for successful job performance. Since the majority of police agencies do not have or cannot afford full-time mental health professionals, outside consultants are used for a variety of psychological services, including the psychological screening of applicants. Outside consultants may be psychologists, psychiatrists, management consultants, and on occasion, physicians. Most often, a licensed professional or certified consultant is required.

An important consideration in choosing a professional for a department is the person's ability to relate to the police organization and to become knowledgeable in police consultation. Police agencies are approached by professionals from all areas and backgrounds who wish to become associated with an agency or propose a project on a fee-for-service or contract basis. In rural areas and small towns, police organizations sometimes develop working arrangements with university professors. In some cases, research academicians look upon police officers as subjects for data-gathering and fail to understand totally the needs of police officers and administrators.

Academic persons working in applied areas or professionals who have done research in areas of police psychology are sometimes better prepared to begin consultation in law enforcement. It is, however, important that such professionals also possess training in the area of identifying clinical or personality issues that could impair police officers' performance. Consultants who are not familiar with the job should approach the consultation task initially as a student, and police agencies should insist on exposing them to relevant areas of police work.

The director or chief of police will often be the primary contact for the consultant. The psychological screening information is usually transmitted directly to him or to another previously designated representative. In most cases, the decision to hire is made by the chief of police after background results, medical results, psychological results, and in some cases, polygraph results are available. Some agencies prefer either a "yes or no" response as to whether an applicant is suitable for police work. This response may be verbal, followed by a written report. Some police administrators prefer to meet with the consultant to discuss each applicant. However, in most cases, a detailed written report including the background as reviewed by the consultant, the results of any psychological tests administered, interview data, and a summary and a recommendation is submitted to the department.

The consultant should function as part of a team that includes all those involved in processing applicants. It is strongly desirable for the consultant to meet with all persons in the system, including the training officers who will eventually complete the screening process by either recommending recruits for permanent status, probation, or termination. The consultant should know the training officer's perspective and be aware of any past psychological problems of the recruits. The training officer should know on what basis the psychologist will recommend marginal applicants be accepted with the hope they will develop as suitable officers during probation.

Consultants should be willing to explain and defend screening decisions should it become necessary. When an applicant appeals a disqualification, the consultant should be available to appear before a civil service board or in court, if necessary.

In many cases, a psychologist or other professional will be hired solely to provide preemployment psychological screening. After the agency develops confidence in him, the consultant may be called upon to perform psychological "fitness for duty" evaluations on officers who have demonstrated patterns of excessive-force complaints or highly unusual or "liability-prone" behavior. Also, officers applying for special assignments, such as bomb squad technicians or hostage negotiators, may be evaluated to ensure that persons chosen are the best suited for the job. In these cases, the officer's personnel file and work history provide valuable information regarding past performance. Information on the number and nature of complaints against the officer, sick time taken, and performance under stress provides valuable input for the psychological consultant.

In all cases, it is important to remember that the decision as to who will be selected for employment and which officers will receive specialized assignments remains in the hands of the administration. The psychologist or consultant only provides specialized information and judgments that will be taken into consideration along with other important factors. In some instances, police administrators may choose officers who have not been recommended by the psychologist. Often, in these instances, the psychological consultant can identify areas of needed development and can suggest to the administration ways of supporting individual development.

Screening Components

Police administrators and managers are often concerned with the validity of psychological tests. Psychological instruments and procedures were developed through scientific and statistical investigation, but the relevance of any single statistical score to a well-integrated psychological judgment is often overemphasized. Good decisions require information. The three best sources of information in evaluating law enforcement applicants are:

1) Psychological tests;

2) Background information; and

3) An indepth or "clinical" interview by a psychologist knowledgeable in law enforcement.

All information developed in the preemployment stages could reasonably be used by a clinical psychologist. Typically, most psychologists choose the Minnesota Multiphasic Personality Inventory (MMPI), the Sixteen Personality Factor Questionnaire (16PF), or the California Psychological Inventory (CPI). Extensive information exists on these instruments and their use in law enforcement screening;[2] however, psychologists may vary in the psychological tests they use depending on their training and experience.

Some psychological tests, such as the MMPI and the 16PF, can be computer scored, but a psychologist must review and interpret the results on an individual basis. Because most computer interpretations of the MMPI are based on the assumption that the test applicant is a mental patient or an outpatient in psychotherapy, negative or pathological information is likely to be emphasized. The MMPI can be extremely useful in screening, but it must be interpreted by a professional who is knowledgeable in both the test's subtleties and law enforcement.

The Psychologist as an Expert Judge

In the psychological screening approach, the psychologist plays a critical role in integrating psychological test results, background information, and interview data in order to arrive at a judgment of unsuitability. This is a "clinical" or expert judgment, not a statistical or scientific outcome. Studies have been done relating various kinds of biographical or psychological test score information to criterion variables, such as disciplinary actions, number of arrests made, commendations, sick time taken, on-the-job automobile accidents, etc. These studies are helpful in suggesting which tests and criteria may be of potential benefit, but to rely totally on test scores and correlations would be inappropriate. It is the psychologist familiar with law enforcement who renders a clinical judgment that brings expertise and credibility to the screening process.

The psychological consultant, properly trained and working as support for management, can maximize the success and professionalism of the screening and selection process.

Psychologists cannot predict the future. However, assuming they know the intricacies of a police officer's job, they can develop relevant information regarding an individual's emotional functioning in a law enforcement position and render a judgment about an individual's suitability. Psychological screening minimizes the admission of inappropriate applicants and is consistent with the safeguards and precautions that the law and commonsense dictate.

About the Authors

Dr. Susan Saxe-Clifford is a specialist in law enforcement psychology. She began with the Los Angeles Police Department where she served on staff for 14 years. Currently she consults for 50 law enforcement agencies in Southern California. She served as consultant to the 1984 Olympic security effort, has published widely in police psychology issues, and is actively involved in professional organizations. Dr. Saxe-Clifford earned her Ph.D. at the University of Southern California in 1974.

Dr. Fabricatore is a police psychologist and management consultant in independent practice. He has worked with major law enforcement and security organizations, including the Los Angeles Police Department, Sheriff's Office and Marshal, as well as the Nuclear Regulatory Commission. A UCLA Ph.D., Dr. Fabricatore's work has been widely published in both the popular and professional press, including Time, Wall Street Journal, Financial Executive *and the* FBI Law Enforcement Bulletin. *An internationally recognized expert, he has presented at numerous symposia, including those sponsored by NATO and the FBI. He also consults with* Fortune 500 *corporations on executive security and security crisis management.*

Footnotes

[1] W.D. Haynes, *Stress Related Disorders in Policemen* (San Francisco: R & E Research Associates, inc., 1978); R.H. Rahe and E.K.E. Gunderson, *Life Stress and Illness* (Springfield, Ill.: Charles C. Thomas, 1974); M. Reiser, "Stress, Distress and Adaptation in Police Work," *The Police Chief,* January 1976.

[2] J. Gottesman, *The Utility of the MMPI in Assessing the Personality Patterns of Urban Police Applicants* (Hoboken: Stevens Institute of Technology, 1975); S.J. Saxe and M. Reiser, "A Comparison of Three Police Applicant Groups Using the MMPI," *Journal of Police Science and Administration,* Vol. 4, No. 4, 1976; J. Fabricatore, F. Azan, and H. Snibbe, "Predicting Performance of Police Officers Using the 16 Personality Factor Questionnaire," *American Journal of Community Psychiatry,* Vol. 6, No. 1, 1978; R.H. Blum, *Police Selection* (Springfield, Ill.: Charles C. Thomas, 1964).

"Psychological Preparation" of Female Police Recruits

By Debra Furman Glaser
and
Susan Saxe

The role of women in law enforcement has changed drama-tically in recent years. In many agencies, the "policewoman" classification no longer exists. Females are hired as "police officers" and are required to meet the same hiring and training criteria as their male counterparts. They are also expected to be able to perform the same law enforcement duties.

In spite of efforts to employ women in patrol duties across the country, the number of women in patrol cars nationwide is low and the average tenure is brief. In addition, police administrators have difficulty recruiting qualified female applicants. Many applicants are unable to pass background and physical agility requirements Of those who enter the academy, a high percentage drop out or are terminated for a myriad of reasons. And those who do reach patrol are quickly transferred to under-cover, juvenile, or administrative assignments where the need for their services is often perceived as greater.

Although the Los Angeles Police Department has had a vigorous program aimed at the recruitment of female officers for several years, a 1980 court-imposed hiring injunction made increasing the percentage of female officers in the department a top priority. However, it soon became obvious that the recruitment of women was only half the battle. The problem of high attrition from the academy had to be addressed.

Statistics revealed that the academy attrition rate for female recruits was 50 percent between 1976 and 1980, as compared to a 17-percent attrition rate for male recruits during the same period. In an effort to resolve this problem, a preliminary program was developed which was aimed at increasing the number of women who would enter the police academy and complete the training program.

The Crime Prevention Assistance Program (CPA) was conceived originally as a "holding pattern" for female recruits. After successfully completing the selection process and while waiting for an academy class to begin, female recruits were put on the payroll and assigned clerical duties in various divisions within the police department. Thus, potential recruits became familiar with department operations, earned money while they waited to enter the academy, and provided a service to the department. Later, a portion of their time was allotted for physical training as preparation for the rigorous academy demands. While this program provided a head start, it soon became apparent, however, that lack of physical ability was not the only or primary reason so many women dropped out. Misconceptions about the police training academy and police work and an unrealistic assessment of the time commitments involved, as well as personal and interpersonal problems unique to female recruits, were all contributing factors to attrition.

As a result, a new and innovative phase of preacademy training was instituted. The department's Behavioral Science Services Section developed and implemented a program designed to address psychological stumbling blocks that prevent women from successfully completing academy training. This program serves as a complement to their physical training regime.

Psychological Stressors

Upon investigation, certain psychological stressors emerged as being particularly disruptive to female police applicants and recruits. Once these stressors were identified and defined, counseling sessions were initiated in order to "psychologically prepare" the CPA women for the police academy and police work.

The Perception of a Woman in a "Man's Job"

Police organizations and law enforcement occupations have been traditionally male. As a result, females sometimes have underlying feelings that their job choice is somewhat inappropriate. Such feelings, often stemming from early sex role identification and socialization, can lead to doubts about competence and self-worth.

Along with questioning the appropriateness of females in police work, in general, many women often question themselves and their individual motivations. The role of a police officer is a difficult and sometimes dangerous role for anyone. A police officer is an authority figure, and in our society, for the most part, authority figures are male. Thus, some women need to reconcile their femininity with their career choice. This issue may also affect a woman's relationship with her spouse and other prominent males in her life. Many men see women as wives, mothers, secretaries, and nurses. They do not see "feminine" women as capable of such a "masculine" job.

A Lack of Support

Compounding the problem is the lack of support they encounter both on and off the job. Husbands, boyfriends, and friends, male or female, may feel threatened by their career choice. Any self-doubt a woman may have will be exacerbated by skeptical friends and police personnel. Despite the overall commitment of police agencies to hire women, some police personnel are less than supportive of this effort and make their feelings known in subtle, and sometimes direct, ways.

Assertiveness

Along with socialization to be "ladylike," we have found that somehow or other ladylike connotes passive and submissive. Such qualities are anathema to police work. Many women need to work on becoming more assertive, that is,

developing authority of voice and stature or developing "command presence."

Romanticism of the Job

Unfortunately, some women are attracted to the job of police officer because they expect police work to be like an adventure as those portrayed on television. Inappropriate or incorrect expectations about job requirements, such as physical training, odd hours, and the quasi-military environment, may result in confusion and even anger.

Two Roles—Recruit and Housekeeper

Many women who enter police academy training continue to assume responsibility for maintaining a home, preparing meals, and child care. By definition, recruit training is more than a full-time job. Recruits must study at home, clean and polish their equipment at home, and keep a schedule which often involves 15-hour days. Traditionally, married male recruits have been able to come home to a prepared meal, clean children, and private time to study. Female recruits are less likely to have partners who will assume housekeeping responsibilities.

Inappropriate Defense Mechanisms

Psychological defense mechanisms are methods used against stress and anxiety. Each person develops a set of defense mechanisms that works for them. Women entering academy training and police work are subject to numerous stressors. In many cases, defense mechanisms that had worked in the past are inappropriate in law enforcement. New approaches must be developed. For example, a female who becomes tearful when under stress would have a difficult time exhibiting command presence with suspects while crying. New methods for defending herself against stressful situations would need to be developed.

Group Counseling

As a means to alleviate the effect of these psychological stressors, weekly 2-hour group counseling sessions were conducted by a psychology intern. The sessions gave the CPA's an opportunity to discuss the identified stressors in confidence and share information on the realities of academy training and police work.

During the 4- to 6-week program, the women were able to discuss feelings about their experiences since becoming a CPA. Typical experiences would include riding with an officer who tells the CPA, "Women shouldn't be cops," or "I don't want a female partner"; negative reactions from family and friends about her new career; or a child's tearful question, "Mommy, are you going to get shot?"

The fostering of group cohesiveness through weekly meetings is an important part of the CPA program. If cohesiveness and mutual support can be maintained throughout academy training, female recruits tend to succeed in greater numbers.

Role playing during group meetings is a valuable tool in allowing the CPA's a preview of how they might respond or what they might feel as a police officer. Scenarios include off-duty situations, such as explaining to a husband specific assignments and overtime obligations. Group confidentiality allows the women to feel comfortable in discussing personal problems. Most often they find they share many feelings.

POWR—Positive Orientation for a Winning Response

The most recent addition to the program is the POWR training. Aimed at relaxation and positive suggestion, the POWR sessions are presented daily for an hour immediately prior to physical training. Audio tapes are played presenting progressive relaxation instructions and suggestions for imagining the successful completion of a task or a proud feeling on graduation day.

The rationale behind the POWR sessions is to help women deal more effectively with the stress and tension that comes with the anticipation of chin-ups and long runs. The tapes were designed specifically for the program. After each session, the tapes are discussed and evaluated for their effectiveness in relieving tension.

Conclusion

Preliminary data for 1981 show a decrease in the attrition rate for female recruits from 50 percent to 7 percent. This substantial decrease after the implementation of the CPA "psychological preparation" program is encouraging. Because of the program's apparent success, a similar program within the LAPD has been planned that will address the relatively high attrition rate of male minorities. In addition, a research project will be designed to evaluate the long term effect of psychological training programs on both academy completion and success in the field.

About the Authors

Debra Furman Glaser, Ph.D. is a staff psychologist with the Los Angeles Police Department. Dr. Glaser currently does clinical work with sworn and civilian members of LAPD, consults with Juvenile Narcotics in the training of their undercover officers, teaches stress management, and functions as a member of the Crisis Negotiation team in SWAT call outs. Dr. Glaser's prior assignment was the development and coordination of the psychological training portion of the Crime Prevention Assistance Program for women at LAPD's police academy. Dr. Glaser received her B.A. from Lehman College in New York, a master's degree from New York University and a master's degree and Ph.D. from the California School of Professional Psychology in Los Angeles. Dr. Glaser has a private practice in Encino, California specializing in the treatment and screening of law enforcement personnel.

Dr. Susan Saxe-Clifford is a specialist in law enforcement psychology. She began with the Los Angeles Police Department where she served on staff for 14 years. Currently she consults for 50 law enforcement agencies in Southern California. She served as consultant to the 1984 Olympic security effort, has published widely in police psychology issues, and is actively involved in professional organizations. Dr. Saxe-Clifford earned her Ph.D. at the University of Southern California in 1974.

CHAPTER II

TRAINING AND DEVELOPMENT

INTRODUCTION TO CHAPTER II:
Training and Development

Once the recruitment process is over, then administrators are faced with their next responsibility: Training and Development. Indeed, recruiting is only part of the formula for effective and efficient law enforcement officers.

In Article 6, Edward J. Tully discusses the role of the training director who is so essential to an effective departmental program. Mr. Tully thoroughly discusses the training director's func- tions as administrator, teacher, advocate and consultant, and finally, as researcher and developer. Clearly, the role of training director, as change agent within a department, is spelled out along with the absolute necessity for good training.

David Nichols argues in Article 7 that small police departments, especially, must take training beyond the minimum standards required by law if they want an excellent organization. Thus, contends Nichols, such departments—as do all departments—must reexamine their training priorities. Nichols also offers some viable suggestions to assist small departments, which make up the majority of this country's law enforcement agencies.

Article 8 logically follows with an overview of the stress caused by the promotional process. Robert Schaefer explains clearly how "devastating" the effects of promotion can be on those officers who were passed over. To help minimize the effects of promotion on passed-over officers, the author offers several practical recommendations that will help any department.

Once supervisors are promoted, agencies are again faced with the training issue. And, Article 9 addresses the issue of training firstline police supervisors. Jack B. Molden, from the Police Training Institute at the University of Illinois, provides a well-constructed and innovative curriculum for any department dedicated to excellent supervisory training. Focused on basic adult-learning principles, often overlooked in training programs, this curriculum employs a strong team concept and an instructional mode which casts the instructor as a facilitator, not a dictator.

The Training Director

By Edward J. Tully

There are few social scientists who would not agree with the fact that the pace of change in American society over the past 25 years has been extremely rapid. In fact, Alvin Toffler in his popular book, *Future Shock,* hypothesized that the change has been too fast for some individuals and institutions in our culture to assimilate. Thus, there has been a certain amount of cultural shock or dysfunction. Whether Toffler is correct or not, all observers agree that there has been rapid social, economic, and political change in America.

On the cutting edge of this change, the professional of law enforcement stood, attempting to preserve order and to be neutral between the competing forces. It was a position which called for considerable immediate change within the profession itself. Law enforcement did not have the luxury of quiet reflection to consider the pros and cons of change. It did not have the time to experiment with alternative solutions to social unrest. Nor was there time for enlightened debate; there was only time for reaction to events. Some reactions were proper and served to preserve order; some were not and only served to inflame the situation. To a certain extent, we are fortunate to have come through this period intact as a profession. To a greater extent, it could be argued that we are more professional for having had the experience.

In this regard, our profession has been well-served by the process of training. In the past 25 years or so, police training programs have substantially increased in quantity, quality, and sophistication. In may cities and States, police are conducting training programs for recruits and in-service personnel, which are the finest of their type in the world. Police training has become, in this relatively short period of time, respectable both in the academic and professional training worlds. If pre-sent trends continue, training will continue to increase its sphere of influence within police organizations in the years to come. In law enforcement circles, at least, the process of training has come of age. Having proved to police administrators and the public the value of strong, responsive training programs, the problem now faced by training managers is to salvage as many of their respective programs as possible in a period of declining or fixed police budgets. This burden, as well as designing new training programs to continue the professionalization of the police, will fall on the training director and his staff.

Just as the process of training has come of age in law enforcement, so has the realization that the position of training director is a demanding, complex, executive position within the agency. In the past, training command used to be a step in the promotional process in law enforcement. Today, a few organizations have realized that this position demands an individual with extensive experience in the design, development, and execution of education and training programs. To understand this trend, let's examine the roles the training director may play within an organization.

A review of literature concerning the role of the training director, including an examination of the subject by Calvin Otto and Rollin Glaser in *The Management of Training,*[1] Leonard Nadler and Gordon Lippit in a 1967 article in the *Training Development Journal,*[2] Leonard Nadler's 1970 book entitled *Developing Human Resources,*[3] and Paul Chaddock's chapter in the second edition of the *Training and Development Handbook,*[4] shows that experts hold the training director functions in the following roles:

1. Administrator of training;

2. Trainer, teacher, philosopher;

3. Advocate or consultant; and

4. Research and development director.

Our experience at the FBI Academy coincides with their findings.

Of course, the training director will not function in all of the above roles simultaneously, and a variety of circumstances within the organization will dictate the amount of time he spends in discharging his responsibilities. Although it is safe to assume that the training director will function primarily as an administrator, he will, over a short period of time, also function in the other roles. In general, then, the overall definition of a training director is, as Nadler suggests, a change agent whose basic goal is to increase organizational effectiveness through the development of the organization's human resources to their maximum potential. Let's examine each specific role in more detail.

Administrator of Training

The primary job of the training director as an administrator is to be aware of the changing function and objectives of the organization. From this position, the administrator also:

1. (a) Determines training needs; (b) prepares goals and objectives; (c) prepares budget; (d) supervises staff selection and evaluation; (e) devises administrative devices and controls; (f) evaluates the effectiveness of training; (g) arranges for material, equipment, and facilities; (h) establishes and maintains a proper learning environment; (i) monitors Government regulations (EEOC, OSHA, etc.); (j) conducts public relations; (k) arranges for faculty development; (l) establishes training policy; and (m) establishes training priorities.

Trainer

As a trainer, philosopher, and perhaps part-time teacher, the training director's primary task is to lead his staff in the design and development of constantly changing curricula relevant to the needs of the organization. The training director may also be expected to:

2. (a) Develop an organizational philosophy of training; (b) select appropriate methods and techniques of instruction; (c) apply learning theory for application to teaching/learning problems; (d) approve terminal performance objectives, lesson plans, and criterion test measures; (e) design specialized training programs; (f) be knowledgeable about developments in the training and development field; and (g) coach the training staff.

Advocate/Consultant

The law enforcement training director must have a broad range of street experience as an officer. This experience, plus his background in training, results in his being considered more frequently as a credible source of advice when the organization faces operational problems. Since many law enforcement problems have either their roots or solution in training, the training director is called upon increasingly to provide answers to complex problems. In addition, in this role the training director may:

3. (a) Advocate change in organizational policy, procedures, or objectives; (b) promote the dissemination of new ideas, equipment, or the wisdom of the status quo; (c) offer advice upon request in tactical situations; and (d) furnish advice on the limitations of training.

Research and Development

In this role, the training director is responsible for the long-range planning of the training function. In a law enforcement agency where change and/or the anticipation of change is a daily event, this is indeed a critical function. The training director must also be prepared to assist in the following areas:

4. (a) Design of organizational research projects; (b) research and development of tactics, weapons, and protective devices; (c) conduct of behaviorally anchored research to be used in the selection of performance appraisal process; and (d) application of behavioral theory to operational practice.

As can be seen from an examination of the above four roles, the position of training director almost demeans an individual who has been professionally prepared for the job. It is becoming doubtful that law enforcement agencies heavily involved in training can much longer afford part-time or non-professional training directors. Since 1960, the number of law enforcement training programs have virtually exploded throughout the Nation. This rapid increase in both quantity and quality of training programs mirrored the increases in the amounts of knowledge and skills needed by recruits to function adequately, the development and implementation of new technology, and new demands on law enforcement's traditional response to social problems.

While it was recognized by law enforcement management that the training process could not solve all problems during this period, training was used more than it had been in the past. The results have been satisfying to all concerned. The fact that the officers today are better trained and educated is tangible proof in the eyes of many experts that law enforcement is more professional in daily operations than ever before. Since it is believed by most social observers that our social problems are going to continue or increase in their diversity and complexity, it would make sense to conclude that law enforcement training programs will become even more specialized and sophisticated. The "architect" of these programs of the future will be the training director. This individual will have to have many qualifications and talents to function effectively in this changing training environment.

The position of director of training within a law enforcement agency almost demands an individual with broad street experience, an extensive background in education and training programs, a strong personality to function as an advocate of new ideas, and the wisdom to act as a teacher, consultant, and confidant. The position also requires administrative skills, research and development skills, and the skill to act as a change agent. Obviously, mere promotion through the ranks will not adequately prepare an individual to serve in this capacity in a modern law enforcement agency. More is needed. Any individual who is chosen to act as training director should be exposed to a wide variety of training experiences, should obtain a strong academic background in adult education, and if possible, should be exposed to training in other parts of the public and private sectors.

The fact that the role of the law enforcement training director is changing apparently parallels the change also occurring in corporate training programs. In the March 1979, issue of the *Training and Development Journal*,[5] Clement, Walker, and Pinto furnished the results of a study of members of the American Society for Training and Development (ASTD). The study was designed to probe the changing demands on the training professional. Over 2,000 trainers responded to the poll and the results indicate that change is occurring in that sector also. While the results cannot be directly applied to law enforcement trainers, the response points to trends which can be expected to have an inevitable impact on our profession. In brief, almost 30 percent of those polled indicated they were spending more time on management duties. Almost 40 percent believed that credibility was the most important behavioral characteristic of the training director. Finally, almost 60 percent of the trainers indicated that "increased technical awareness" and "increased knowledge of the behavioral sciences" were emerging as important requirements for the training and development professional.

It is realized that the above results are subject to wide interpretation as to their meaning and possible conclusion. But the results tend to confirm our observations of the law enforcement training process at the FBI Academy. That is, the role of the training director as an administrator at both the State and local levels is increasing. The increasing use of educational technology, best exemplified by the recruit training programs of the Los Angeles Police Department and the Metropolitan Police in Washington, D.C., demands a high level of technical expertise on the part of the training director. Newly developed crisis intervention, hostage negotiation, and criminal behavior courses demand a thorough knowledge of the behavioral sciences. Finally, the issue of credibility of the training director in law enforcement is critical to the continued use of the training process to solve organizational problems. There is a time to train and a time when training will not solve the problem. Knowing the difference is important and having the credibility within the organization to sell the difference is critical.

Conclusion

If law enforcement agencies are going to be receptive to the impact of change in either individuals or institutions in our society, we must be prepared to use the training process as a means to assist both individuals and institutions to cope with change. The identification of training as one means by which an organization can solve problems is important, but finding an individual within the organization to develop and retain as the manager of this process is more important. Clearly, what we need is a "man of all season." It is not easy to find such an individual to act as the training director, but the effort will pay rich dividends in the long run.

About the Author

Edward J. Tully has been assigned at the FBI Academy, Quantico, Virginia, since 1972. He served as an instructor in the Education/Communication Arts Unit, administrator of the In-Service Program, administrator of Institutional Research, and was named Chief of the Education/Communication Arts Unit in 1978. Since 1976, he has been the Program Administrator of the National Executive Institute, which is an executive training program for the chief executives of our nation's largest law enforcement organizations. Prior to his assignment at the FBI Academy, SA Tully served in the Richmond Division and the Tampa Division. Mr. Tully received his Master of Science in Public School Administration from Illinois State University and served as a public school administrator for four years prior to his appointment as a Special Agent of the FBI in 1962.

He has written numerous articles on law enforcement education, police/media relations, and future trends in law enforcement.

Footnotes

[1] Calvin Otto and Rollin Glaser, *The Management of Training* (Reading, Mass.: Addison-Wesley Company, 1970), pp. 3-11.

[2] Gordon L. Lippit and Leonard Nadler, "Emergency Roles of the Training Director," *Training and Development Journal,* August 1967, Vol. 21, No. 8.

[3] R. L. Craig (Ed.), *Training and Development Handbook,* 2d ed. (New York: McGraw-Hill, 1976), chapter 3, pp. 1-4.

[4] Leonard Nadler, *Developing Human Resources* (Houston: Gulf Publishing Co., 1970) *passim.*

[5] Donald Clement, Patrick Pinto, and James Walker, "Changing Demands on the Training Professional," *Training and Development Journal,* March 1979, Vol. 33, No. 3, pp. 3-7.

Beyond Minimum Standards:
Staff Development for Small Police Departments

By David Nichols

Every police department should implement and maintain an employee development program designed to further the on-the-job growth of employees. While most large police departments operate separate training divisions and formal training programs for personnel development, they represent only a small percentage of the number of police departments in this country.

There are approximately 18,000 law enforcement agencies in the United States. Of this number, 50 percent have less than 10 officers and 80 percent have less than 25 officers.[1] This indicates where the emphasis on training is needed—in small departments. Yet, small departments may often find it difficult to fulfill the responsibilities of an effective staff development program.

Numerous constraints face the police chief of the small department, one of which is the number of sworn personnel in the department. If the entire organization consists of 10 members, then sending 2 officers for advance training would create a manpower shortage. Another area of concern is the funds available to support staff development activities. Many smaller department's political subdivisions do not actively support the continuing education, training, and development of their police officers.[2] Also, while an inhouse development program may be an alternative, some police administrators do not have qualified instructors or a plan for such a program. Yet, there exists a definite need for viable staff development programs in small police departments.

Today, all States except Hawaii require minimum standards training for entry-level police officers.[3] Under the Alabama Minimum Standards and Training Act of 1972, all police officers or peace officers in the State are required to receive a minimum number of training hours—currently 280 hours.[4] These efforts have served to upgrade the quality and performance of police officers. However, it is becoming increasingly evident that the individual police employee must be afforded continuous development opportunities to be effective and enhance job performance. The influx of intelligent, inquisitive, and social-conscious young officers serves to emphasize the need for education and training. In may instances, these officers have been exposed to the college environment and desire to continue their education after entering law enforcement. The advent of college-trained/educated officers serves to emphasize the need for training.[5] Minimum standards aren't enough.

Society's increased awareness of crime, its subsequent demand for better services, and its misconceptions about the police require that the quality of personnel be improved.[6] It is imperative that police officers receive adequate training to keep pace with our fast-changing technological society. As times change, so do problems and their complexity. In order to ensure the preparedness and effectiveness of small police departments, their personnel must be involved in continuous professional development beyond minimum standards training.

The chief administrator has the main responsibility for staff development, which is closely linked to the expectations of the general public. If the general public expects a certain level of performance, then police personnel must be equipped to fulfill this expectation. In meeting these responsibilities, the chief administrator should have certain objectives in mind. The training function should be viewed as a process whereby the organization can aid its members in becoming more effective in their present or future positions. Training not only improves and increases the skills and knowledge of individual officers but also improves the efficiency and proficiency of the organization as a whole.

Many police chiefs are faced with training personnel while staying within their budgets. Too often, administrators send officers to school arbitrarily, without any plan or purpose in mind. Consequently, they often run low or out of funds before training the expected number of personnel is completed.

Planning is essential to the operation of any organization, and when feasible, the chief administrator should appoint a training officer to lead in the planning and implementation.[7] A training program must be included in planning decisions as well as budget proposals. One relatively novel approach is policing by objective (PBO), which involves every aspect of the police organization. An integral part of the PBO approach is a comprehensive staff development/training program incorporating input from all members of the organization. Subsequently, the end result should meet the needs of the organization as expressed by its members.[8]

Inservice training is only a part of a comprehensive staff development program; yet, it is a very significant component. There are various traditional approaches to inservice training and education, most of which can be used by the small police department. It is important to include all personnel in some training activities, i.e., dispatchers, investigators, clerical staff, and patrol officers. Regularly scheduled training sessions using films, tapes, guest speakers, and/or training officers are well-accepted methods and are particularly adaptable to the small department. The FBI provides qualified instructors to conduct training sessions for local police departments at no cost, and professional police associations, such as the International Association of Chiefs of Police sponsor a wide range of training workshops, seminars, conferences, and programs. In addition, training bulletins, both in-house and external, are excellent to keep officers abreast of professional development, innovative techniques, and changing laws.

Coach-pupil training, if planned and done correctly, can also produce rewards for the small department. For example, a supervisor may ride with a subordinate during a shift and teach vehicle stop techniques or patrol techniques. Staff meetings or general department meetings are often convenient means to provide special training for personnel, as

are seminars, conferences, and workshops. The latter may involve travel and leave time, but will prove rewarding as a motivational factor.

Many smaller departments use nearby college criminal justice departments as resources, while others pool their resources and establish joint training sessions with neighboring police departments. Campus police departments have also recently made strides in inservice training programs to complement minimum standards in training. In 1980, the Alabama Association of College and University Police Administrators sponsored the first statewide training seminar for campus police/security officers.[9]

A relatively new training technique, which works especially well for smaller departments, is the use of the video recording system. Many educational films and materials are available through State and regional film libraries for a nominal fee. The time spent viewing the tapes, films, etc., is minimal and can be done on duty or roll call time, thus avoiding both overtime costs, travel, lodging costs, etc. A positive feature of this approach is the ability of the small department to produce its own training programs as well as public relations materials.

The application of computer technology is constantly expanding. So why not use this medium for inservice training? This departs from the traditional teacher-learner method and offers some advantages. The courseware can be developed by the department and adapted to the specific needs of the individual. This has already proven effective in college criminal justice courses. While the initial costs may be somewhat high, they are minimized by the long-range benefits. This is also the least expensive medium when considering the cost of training personnel.[10]

There are certainly other innovative techniques for inservice training programs. In fact, the possibilities are as broad as the creativity of the chief administrator and the instructional staff. Many methods and techniques can be adapted or developed by the small department to meet its own needs. What is important is to maintain an effective inservice training program beyond minimum standards requirements.

In the 1970's, universities responded to the needs of the police by initiating academic programs where none existed. These universities have become more flexible in providing undergraduate and graduate programs to meet the needs of these "student" cops.

Today, numerous university programs for educating and training police officers are available. Police training at this educational level reduces to a very marked degree the load on inservice training, but does not take its place. Both are necessary.[11] Since many police officers now enter the law enforcement profession with college degrees, other officers are influenced to continue their education. They recognize the importance of higher education in a society where the level of education is steadily rising.

Higher education can also develop qualities of leadership and executive potential. It will give officers a long-range perspective of the role of the police in modern society. College training is important for competitive reasons, and this is becoming increasingly true in the area of law enforcement.

Staff development in small police departments often focuses on training, educating, and improving the rank-and-file patrol officers, while overlooking the continuous improvement of the police manager. The challenges of managing police departments can be met only by dedicated professionals who possess the knowledge and experience to participate in the broad issues of the day. Because police managers are held to a higher degree of accountability, they must improve their command of management skills and techniques. Police managers must be given adequate tools if they are to perform properly, and the inclusion of executive education in developing managerial resources can make a special contribution to the management capacity of police executives and their sponsoring agencies. "Police schools" will not be enough to prepare a police manager to meet the challenges of the 1980's. Subsequently, it is important to give police managers and potential police managers the opportunity to grow professionally by taking advantage of professional courses in management.[12]

Staff development for the small police department should be viewed as a comprehensive approach which goes beyond inservice training and college police education programs. The development of the officers in other areas will enhance their total effectiveness. Often, training and education do not provide the job satisfaction and motivation all employees need. There are other approaches which can improve personnel.

Personnel rotation is an effective means of employee development. In smaller departments, rotation may be limited to geographic areas of varying crime incidence and major functional assignments. This offers employees new and valuable perspectives on work and responsibility. Lateral transfers to other job assignments may also be an incentive, as well as a method for further developing the employee's experience, knowledge, skills, and perspective. Promotion is an ideal method of developing employees as they grow professionally and become proficient at each level.[13]

Special assignments and/or extra responsibility are often good methods for improving and developing an employee. This shows the employee the administrator's confidence in him/her and affords the employee the opportunity to demonstrate skills and abilities. This is particularly feasible in a small department where responsibilities can be shared among rank-and-file employees due to the lack of organizational specialization.

Another area which merits attention is personal counseling for police personnel. Stress is a proven factor relating to performance among police officers. Special sessions could be held, collectively or individually, to address such issues as conflict resolution, marital difficulties, anxiety, stress, etc.

Summary

Minimum standards requirements represent only the tip of the iceberg. It is essential that police administrators recognize the significance of a continuous, comprehensive staff development program for their department no matter how large or how small. To fail to recognize this and respond effectively will result in a stagnant, ineffective police organization full of disgruntled, non-productive individuals. Surely, a well-trained force will be more motivated than an ill-trained one. To be committed to quality training and staff development will yield bountiful fruits of a motivated and productive department.[14] Above all, the organization will gain public support because citizens will recognize the results in terms of improved performance, motivated officers, and a more professional posture.

About the Author

David Nichols is the Director of Public Safety at Jacksonville State University in Jacksonville, Alabama where he also serves as an adjunct instructor in the College of Criminal Justice. Dr. Nichols holds a bachelor's degree in Political Science and a master's degree in School Administration from the University of Montevallo. In 1985 he earned a Doctor of Education degree from the University of Alabama. He has authored numerous journal articles and has written a book entitled The Administration of Public Safety in Higher Education *(1987).*

Footnotes

[1] J.V. Cotter, Commission on Accreditation for Law Enforcement Agencies. Presentation at the Alabama Association of Chiefs of Police Conference, February 13, 1984.

[2] J.H. Auten, *Training in the Small Department* (Springfield, Ill.: Charles C. Thomas, 1973), pp. 5-6.

[3] Supra note 1.

[4] D. Nichols, "Campus Police: The New Professionals," *American School and University,* Vol. 52, 1979, p. 72.

[5] Supra note 2, pp. 7-8.

[6] C.B. Saunders, *Upgrading the American Police* (Washington, D.C.: The Brookings Institute, 1970), p. 33.

[7] G.R. Bandics, "Department Training Officers and the Training Process," *FBI Law Enforcement Bulletin,* Vol. 50, No. 4, April 1981, pp. 12-15.

[8] V.A. Lubans and J.M. Edgar, *Policing by Objectives* (Hartford, Conn.: Social Development Corp., 1978), p. 178.

[9] D. Nichols, "Public Safety on Campus," *FBI Law Enforcement Bulletin,* Vol. 51, No. 10, October 1982, pp. 19-23.

[10] R.O. Walker, "Training: A Rationale Supporting Computer Based Instruction," *The Police Chief,* Vol. 49, 1982, pp. 60-64.

[11] V.A. Leonard and H.W. More, *Police Organization and Management* (Mineola, N.Y.: The Foundation Press, 1978), p. 351.

[12] A.J. Schembri, "Educating Police Managers," *The Police Chief,* Vol. 50, 1983, pp. 36-38.

[13] P.B. Weston and P.K. Fraley, *Police Personnel Management* (Englewood Cliffs, N.J.: Prentice-Hall, Inc., 1980), pp. 116-117.

[14] G.P. Gallagher, "Productivity and Motivation in Training: It is up to you, boss," *The Police Chief,* Vol. 50, 1983, pp. 101-102.

The Stress of Police Promotion

By Robert B. Schaefer

The concept of competitive promotion is relatively new in the criminal justice system. Prior to organized law enforcement, the head of a family, tribe, or clan assumed a position of authority. Later, sheriffs and constables were appointed by the crown, governor, or finally, by popular election.[1] This led to the birth of "politics" within police systems. The police officer who had the most personal influence or who was willing to pay the highest price for promotion was raised to the next highest grade.[2] Today, promotions are based on testing, interviews, and analyses of ability and performance. As a result, the promotional process imposes unique stressors upon police officers.

Stress, in general terms, can be defined as the amount of wear and tear on the human body caused by living.[3] Police work has been traditionally referred to as an occupation that leads to a variety of stress-related maladies, such as hypertension, cardiovascular irregularities, and gastrointestinal disorders.[4] This is probably due, in part, to the actual physical dangers associated with being a police officer.

The law enforcement profession, however, creates other stresses, less physical in nature, but equally wearing. These emotional stressors stem from the ingestion and "burying alive" of undigested everyday negative stress, also known as distress. This distress, inherent in the internal and external environmental demands made upon police officers, modifies their behavior. Among the least explored areas of this distress is the stress associated with promotion and career development. Such stress can be negative (distress) or positive (eustress), depending upon the individual's ability to keep the stress within his individual tolerance or elastic limits. This limit varies from individual to individual. If an individual does recognize this limit, stress can be used to his advantage in the career development and promotional system.

The first stressor to be considered and understood in modern police career development systems is the awareness that organizational charts are hierarchical and paramilitary—there is very little room at the top. There are more police officers than sergeants, more sergeants than lieutenants, etc.[5] This fact is frequently ignored or overlooked by employees and management officials, and as a consequence, becomes a source of severe stress for many officers. Phil Caruso, President of the New York City Police Department Patrolmen's Benevolent Association, recently stated, "The department no longer wants seasoned senior people doing the headquarters jobs, and there is little or no promotion."[6] This stressor is, in part, responsible for reports of spiraling retirements reaching 2,026 for the fiscal year ending June 30, 1982, in New York City.[7] These officers are seeking alternatives for what Caruso has labeled "a deadend job."[8]

A second stressor is the promotional examination process. Civil service laws in most cities provide that promotions be made through successive ranks. Promotional examinations are open only to those who have served in the next lower rank for a specified period of time.

The written examination is usually prepared by either the Office of Personnel Management (formerly the Civil Service Commission) or the department itself to test a candidate's knowledge and understanding of subject matter required for a new position. Normally, an officer's educational background does not play a significant role in promotion, except as it contributes to the acquisition of "test-taking ability," which permits his moving up the promotional ladder at an accelerated rate.

Traditionally, promotional examinations have had few, if any, questions pertaining to the measurement of general management concepts.[9] This generates frustration among police officers who believe that

47

handle particular positions, rather than on a test of memory and reading skills. Police officers should be promoted because they are competent to carry out the functions and tasks demanded by the particular ranks for which they are competing.[10] All too often, as a result of the ability to do well on tests, one falls prey to the "Peter Principle." The "Peter Principle" in a police hierarchy emerges when an employee tends to rise to his level of incompetence.[11] A common assumption made in the law enforcement profession is that an individual who performs well as a sergeant will perform equally as well as a lieutenant and so forth. However, experience has demonstrated that this is not necessarily true.[12]

The written examinations police officers "cram" for are a continuing source of frustration for police officers. They are usually the chief factor in determining promotion. Using the written test to measure management skills, such as planning, organizing, and leadership, severely limits some officers.[13] A recent study of the promotional methods of 10 law enforcement agencies reflected that respondents felt frustrated by the use of a single selection instrument.[14] Their frustration is easily recognizable in the following comments:

"Written tests only measure ability to retain study material."

"The written exam did not test true knowledge of my profession. In our case the officer with the best memorization capabilities has the best chance for promotion."

"No written exam can evaluate potential, judgment, or commonsense."

"I completed only the written test and I feel that no written test can evaluate a person's supervisory capabilities. . . ."[15]

Officers often become obsessed with the written examination. Paradoxically, this worry affects their efficiency and performance. The level of stress tends to increase with the announcement of a promotional examination within a department.[16] Although this stress can be healthy if properly directed, when taken to extremes, it can upset the relationships of an entire police department.

The written examination is usually followed by an interview conducted by three or more high-ranking departmental officers. The next step is the preparation of a special or promotional performance rating for each candidate. These performance ratings frequently include subjective items such as reliability, dependability, job attitude, and quality of work. Supplementary criteria such as work products, education, citations, physical and medical condition, disciplinary action, and veterans' credit may be interwoven into the performance rating or given special consideration.[17]

When the examinations and ratings are completed and the candidates are listed in the order in which they have passed, the appointing authority of the police department is generally given the opportunity of selecting one out of every three names presented to him from the top of the list for every vacancy available.[18]

The creation and publication of the promotional list is a significant stressor. The long term effects on the self-esteem of those officers passed over, yet considered qualified by examination standards for the vacant position, are devastating. In addition, Equal Employment Opportunity (EEO) court decisions have frozen promotional lists across the United States in cities such as Atlanta, Boston, Chicago, Los Angeles, Memphis, New Orleans, and New York.[19] Organizational stress mounts and departments experience the needless loss of highly competent, trained, experienced officers to other law enforcement agencies or even to other professions.

Promotional opportunities often occur during the midlife emotional crisis in a person's life cycle. Thus, the officer is competing at a time when he is already experiencing personal stress. These stages of development for both men and women have been identified and addressed by both Yale social psychologist Daniel Levinson[20] and author Gail Sheehy.[21] The developmental stage most likely to affect those in career development has been called the midlife emotional crisis. This typically occurs in both males and females between the ages of 35 and 42,[22] although it can occur earlier or later in life. This period presents an individual with predictable challenges, crises, and problems that must be resolved. If this individual is already experiencing stress as a result of participation in the career development program and is several managerial levels below where he or she expected to be, the midlife crisis can intensify this career development stress. Without recognition and understanding of this stage, this stress can lead to feelings of apathy or to a pattern of blaming one's failure on others or the system.

Recommendations

Stressors for those involved in the career development program will never be eliminated, but certain logical steps may be taken to keep stress within one's own tolerance limits. Police executives throughout the United States should examine their department's promotional policies to determine whether their policies are realistic in terms of modern police organizations. Executives should also examine the entire system to ensure it has been designed to operate in a manner that will *reduce* rather than *induce* stress. The administrator needs to ask himself, "Have I, as an administrator, determined the best method for identifying the specific competencies associated with positions and ranks?" Only after the administrator has discovered what these specific competencies are, can they be measured.[23] Written tests have been challenged, and promotional lists permit contamination by "politics" or "palace guards." One method for reducing test and list stress is the implementation of assessment centers to choose supervisory and management personnel.

The administrators of the Metropolitan Police Department (MPD), Washington, D.C., have recognized and are actively attempting to minimize promotional stress by standardization and removal of subjectivity from promotions up to and including the rank of captain. Their new promotional examination system consists of a written examination to test knowledge and a performance-based phase to test management skills. The written examinations are made up by MPD sworn personnel. Inclusion of EEO officers in the promotional system from the outset provides guidance and prevents affirmative action issues from arising.[24]

In Chicago, Ill., psychologist William Ruch has developed an assessment center entitled "What Now Sergeant?"[25] Candidates for promotion are observed during an inbasket exercise to rate their ability to manage time and prioritize work. Additionally, the candidates participate in simulated exercises to rate their ability to react as a manager when there is no "operational cookbook" available to cover the varying situations that arise. The cities of Memphis, New Orleans, Richmond, and Rochester are also using assessment centers for the selection of promotional candidates. Traditional multiple choice and essay-type examinations have not been favorably received by the courts, while the opposite has been true of assessment centers.[26]

It is also important for the individual officer to learn to take personal inventory of himself. This includes asking three important questions: Who am I? Where am I going? and Why? The next step is to move at his own pace, carrying with him an awareness of the stressors to which he is likely to be exposed. Learning to visualize several alternatives may also assist an officer in surmounting those inevitable, uncontrollable, organizational barriers toward upward mobility.

Stressors for officers participating in the career development program are both numerous and varied. They begin with the organizational structure of police departments and are further complicated by written and oral examinations, court decisions, and even the officer's self-induced stress. Police executives have begun to recognize these unique stressors. Future efforts are being directed toward *reducing* rather than *inducing* promotional stress. The use of assessment centers within police departments to replace the traditional written examination represents a positive step in that direction.

About the Author

Bob Schaefer is a Supervisory Special Agent of the Federal Bureau of Investigation (FBI) and now serves as the Supervisor for the Organized Crime, Criminal and Drug Squad for the FBI's Norfolk, Virginia Office. Formerly an Instructor at the FBI Academy in both the Management Science and Behavioral Science Units, Mr. Schaefer taught management to Bureau officials and sociology, stress and post-critical incident reactions in the National Academy. He was cofounder and first Program Manager for the FBI's Post-Critical Incident/ Peer Support Program and an Adjunct Professor at the University of Virginia. Mr. Schaefer holds a B.A. degree in Sociology/Psychology from Queens College and an M.P.A. from John Jay College of Criminal Justice, both in New York City, New York. He is the author of numerous articles and pam-

phlets including a pamphlet distributed to all FBI Agents and used as a model for local law enforcement agencies entitled, Shooting Incidents: Issues and Explanations for FBI Agents and Managers.

Footnotes

[1] National Advisory Commission on Criminal Justice Standards and Goals. *Task Force on Police* (Washington, D.C.: U.S. Government Printing Office, 1973), p. 6.

[2] Leonard Felix Fuld, *Police Administration: A Critical Study of Police Organizations in the U.S. and Abroad* (New York: G.P. Putnam and Sons, 1909), p. 425. (Though dated, this text provides an instructive and valuable overview of the development of police organizations.)

[3] Hans Selye, *The Stress of Life* (New York: McGraw-Hill Book Company, 1978), p. 1.

[4] J.J. Hurrell and W.H. Kroes, "Stress Awareness," *Job Stress and The Police Officer: Identifying Stress Reduction Techniques* (Washington, D.C.: U.S. Department of Health, Education and Welfare, 1975).

[5] J.R. McCall, "Promoting Competent Police Officers," *The Police Chief*, November 1981, p. 54.

[6] Jerry Schmetterer and Stuart Marques, "Police Exodus Soaring," *New York Daily News*, December 3, 1981, p. 8.

[7] Ibid.

[8] Ibid.

[9] Lawrence R. O'Leary, *The Successful Police Officer* (Springfield: Charles C. Thomas, Inc., 1979), pp. 79-80.

[10] Supra note 5.

[11] Ibid.

[12] Peter D. Bullard, *Coping With Stress: A Psychological Survival Manual* (Portland: Pro-Seminar Press, 1980), p. 164.

[13] Supra note 9.

[14] John F. Miller, "The Police Promotional Process," *The Police Chief*, November 1981, p. 52.

[15] Ibid.

[16] Ibid., p. 53.

[17] Sidney Epstein and Richard S. Layman, *Guidelines For Police Performance and Placement Procedures* (Washington, D.C.: U.S. Department of Justice, 1973), p. 28.

[18] Ibid.

[19] Marc Levinson, "Affirmative Action: Enforcing New Priorities," March 1982, pp. 17-19.

[20] Daniel J. Levinson with C.N. Darrow, E.B. Klein, M.H. Levinson, and B. McKee, *The Seasons of a Man's Life* (New York: Alfred A. Knopf, Inc., 1978).

[21] Gail Sheehey, *Passages: Predictable Crises in Adult Life* (New York: Bantam Books Edition, 1977).

[22] Daniel J. Levinson, Charlotte N. Darrow, Edward B. Klein, Maria H. Levinson, Braxton McKee, "Periods in the Adult Development of Men: Ages 18 to 45," *Counseling Psychologist*, Vol. 6, No. 1, 1976, p. 21.

[23] Supra note 5.

[24] Ronald E. Crytzer, David Faison, Jr., Max J. Krupo, Thomas Novak, Fred W. Raines, Jimmie L. Wilson, "Promotion Process," *The Police Chief*, January 1981, p. 44.

[25] Supra note 20.

[26] Ibid.

Training Firstline Police Supervisors: A New Approach

By Jack B. Molden

It was 7:58 a.m., Monday morning. As the students found their name cards, they seated themselves around the U-shaped table. The talk was laconic, glances guarded and cool. At the podium, framed by the green chalkboard, the instructor readied his notes, oblivious for the moment to the wandering, shuffling, and quizzical glances of the incoming, casually attired students. A few of the younger arrivals moved with an air of familiarity and casualness in the classroom environment, the older men moved with some obvious trepidation—slow, cautious, unsure. At exactly 8:00 a.m., the vested, somewhat formidable looking instructor called the class into session with the greeting, "Good morning, men. Welcome to the first offering of the all new firstline supervisor course."

Since September 4, 1979, there have been eight offerings of the "new and improved" firstline supervision course by the Police Training Institute. The course has been revised and approved by the Illinois State Training Board, and about 180 officers have been trained and returned to their departments.

What preceded this first course—the commitment, the procedures, the problems, and some solutions—should be of interest and assistance to other trainers, supervisors, and law enforcement managers.

The Police Training Institute

The Police Training Institute is a unit of the University of Illinois at Urbana/Champaign, legally mandated and fully committed to training Illinois law enforcement officers.

For over 25 years, the institute has trained officers from departments of varying sizes in skills ranging from basic law enforcement to executive management. The faculty and staff consist of 40 full-time personnel, teaching a range of over 20 different courses.

New Curriculum Needed

Police supervision has, for many years, been taught at the Police Training Institute. Because of the critical role played by the firstline law enforcement supervisor and the impact of that role on the operation of an agency, supervisory training occupied a high priority at the institute. The course had been offered in the traditional lecture mode, was well attended, and was generally accepted by the students, although it had been recognized for some time that major changes and updating were needed.

The preliminary search for an acceptable curriculum model for supervisory training began in 1977, but a final decision for change was not acted upon until early 1979, when the director and several interested staff members met and decided on overall program goals. The decision to design a completely new course was made at that time. Two staff members accepted responsibility for the design and preparation of the curriculum.

Having failed to identify an acceptable model for the new course, it was decided that one would have to be written. Current literature and courses of instruction were reviewed, and guidance from both staff and police practitioners was sought in developing a curriculum philosophy.

Philosophical Concepts

In an attempt to devise guidelines for curriculum development, the following philosophical concepts were adopted:

1) The traditional lecture, instructor-centered mode of instruction would be minimized and emphasis would be placed on the perfor-

mance-oriented instructional method. This teaching mode would give the students an opportunity to practice what they learned while still in the instructional environment.

2) The course of instruction would be directed toward the novice firstline supervisor, who would attend the class either shortly before or shortly after promotion to a supervisory rank.

3) The course content would exclude all extraneous "nice to know" information and focus, instead, on basic supervisory skills.

4) An instructional "team" approach would provide for maximum coordination and instructional continuity.

Curriculum Development

The most difficult problem initially encountered was determining what material could and should be taught in a 2-week course that would be pertinent to supervisors from all sizes of departments operating under different leadership and management styles. The primary question seemed to be what factors, if any, were common to all firstline police supervisors. Once those factors were determined, it was necessary to design an effective method of teaching that common information.

The answer to this question appeared to be based on a common definition of a supervisor—"one who accomplishes work and meets goals and objectives through the efforts of other people." If that definition is correct, one common factor all supervisors deal with is people. Therefore, all extraneous materials not dealing directly with the officer as a supervisor was extracted, and the content of the course was centered around improving the officer's ability to supervise—it is a people-related course. Each block of instruction is designed to help the supervisor understand his relationship to people, sometimes in relation to a particular police function.

The course ultimately totaled 79 hours of instruction presented in 2 weeks. (See fig. 1.)

Course Organization

Recognizing that each instructional unit is an integral part of the whole course, proper sequencing of the instructional blocks to provide a natural flow

FIGURE 1

COURSE OUTLINE

Administrative Units (11 Hours)	Hours
Introduction and Orientation	2
Comprehensive Practical Examination	4
Examination	2
Critique/Evaluation/Graduation	3

Instructional Units (42 hours)	
Authority and Control	2
Characteristics and Qualities of Leadership	2
Contemporary Issues in Supervision	4
Decisionmaking	2
Measuring Work Performance and Employee Efficiency	2
Morale and Discipline	2
Patrol Supervision	2
Preparing Goals and Objectives	2
Principles of Communication	4
Psychological Aspects of Supervision	4
Short Range Planning and Work Assignment	3
Supervisor's Role in Handling Complaints and Grievances	2
The Supervisor's Role in Management	3
The Supervisor's Training Function	6
The Supervisory Process	2

Practicals (26 hours)	
Complaints and Grievances Practical	2
Comprehensive Practical Exercise	2
Discipline Practical	2
Evaluation Practical	3
Patrol Practical	2
Planning and Decisionmaking Practical	3
Practical Teaching—Coach-Pupil	4
Practical Teaching—Roll Call	4
Principles of Communication Practical	4
TOTAL HOURS	**79**

of information became a critical concern. It was necessary for the sequence to form a building block effect toward the understanding of supervision. Since blocks of instruction had to be shared among several instructors, continuity also became a concern. How could one instructor build on the previous instruction and lead into the following subject when he was familiar with and interested in only his own subject matter? In most instructional courses where multiple instructors are used, this natural defect is considered a necessary evil.

However, we believed that it was imperative that we improve on the traditional delivery mode and resolve this conflict. The instructional "team" approach seemed to be an ideal solution to our problem.

The Team Approach

Staffing the course began with finding four faculty members with expertise in supervision and management, who were willing to become generalists regarding the entire 79-hour course. They committed themselves to coordinating their material with other instructors, adopting common words, terms, definitions and theories, and becoming familiar with the total course content. They also committed themselves to unusually demanding workloads because of the small group teaching style.

Four qualified staff members were found, and the course began with their commitment to monitor the entire course. Because of this commitment by the staff, the course became a true team effort, albeit a time-consuming and tedious one.

An interesting side result of the presence of all four instructors in the classroom during the initial pilot offering was a warm rapport and camaraderie between staff and students that has not been duplicated. The students responded in a very positive manner to the opportunity to relate to instructors informally and to see them participating on a regular basis in the classroom routine.

The team teaching approach has unquestionably been the greatest contributor to the success of the course. Because of other teaching commitments and personal requirements, however, it has been impractical to maintain the original team of four; two additional team members have been added.

Instructional Mode

Performance orientation requires the student to become involved in the instruction in a very significant way. He is allowed to apply his newly acquired skills and knowledge to simulated situations.

For example, a 2-hour block of instruction on morale and discipline is followed by a 2-hour practical exercise where students roleplay in a disciplinary scenario and have an opportunity to both put the principles to use and to see the results. A 2-hour block of instruction in patrol supervision is followed by a 2-hour problem in which the students are broken into four groups of six and given a manpower allocation and distribution problem that is applied to a major case study problem. Another block of instruction, supervisors training function, is followed by student preparation of instructional objectives and lesson plans and the actual teaching of two blocks of instruction—one using the coach/pupil method and the other, roleplay training which is videotaped. During all stages of instruction, student performance is critiqued by a faculty member.

Performance-oriented instruction is far superior to the traditional lecture method, but application of the method requires several components:

1) To allow for adequate student participation, class size must be reduced. Our classes are restricted to 24 students, although a limit of 20 students would probably be better.

2) Performance-oriented instruction requires much more time than the lecture method. However, the additional time used for roleplaying, case studies, and problem solving makes the instruction more meaningful—learning takes place and behavior is changed.

3) Students should be seated in the classroom so they can see and communicate with one another. Although a horseshoe configuration is sometimes used, a semicircle would be preferable when space allows.

4) "Break-out" rooms for practical small group work are another necessity. These are small rooms in which a group of six students solve problems without undue disturbance from others.

5) A much higher ratio of staff-to-student is needed. We typically use four instructors in all small group sessions—about one instructor to six students. It is also important that all instructors understand the material and evaluate student performance on a standardized basis.

6) While working closely with students in small groups in a problem-solving mode is a rewarding experience for the instructor, it is also the most difficult style of teaching and requires a depth of knowledge and skill not needed in an instructor-centered, lecture method of teaching.

Testing

Although testing has been retained for the purpose of feedback and student performance evaluation, traditional paper and pencil tests have been minimized and evaluation of observable behavior through roleplaying, simulation, and case study has been maximized.

There is a total of 100 evaluation points available to the student over the 2-week class period. A possible 55 points are awarded for the performance of practical problems, while there are only a possible 45 points for written tests.

The planned learning sequence is to teach the skill or principle, have the student perform the skill or apply the principles, then critique and evaluate the student's performance. Feedback to the student in the form of a critique and a number grade is immediate.

Students record their grades, and as the course progresses, are able to determine their score or grade at any time.

Central City Case Study

During orientation, students are given a copy of the Central City Case Study. This is a profile of a medium-sized police department, with accompanying statistics and facts. The class, divided into four equal study groups, is requested to apply daily instructional principles and concepts to the solution of the case study problem. A considerable amount of time is spent by these groups in applying information, making decisions, and solving problems posed by the study. On the final day of the course, each group reports their solution to the problem to the entire class. Each group's performance is evaluated by a panel of instructors and a group grade is awarded, based on the group's ability to apply theories and concepts learned in class.

The case study exercise not only forces the students to apply their newly acquired knowledge and skills but also requires the student supervisors to learn to work together creatively to solve common problems. The exercise provides a common thread throughout the course, and student solutions and presentations have been of surprisingly good quality, demonstrating considerable mastery of course material.

Course Textbook

The decision whether to use a course textbook was difficult. One difficulty associated with using a textbook in the presentation of a short course is the obligation to adopt the general organization, definitions, and concepts of the text. This obligation often creates conflicts, particularly when different instructors teach the course. Each instructor, an authority in his own right, has usually developed unique methods of teaching a subject and finds it unduly confining to tailor his material to correspond with a textbook. Conversely, and equally important, it is virtually impossible to find a text that closely corresponds with the material one wishes to offer.

A textbook used in conjunction with a short course, if properly selected and used, provides organization as well as a background reading source, a coordinating effect between the instructors, and common definitions, examples, and concepts.

Research soon disclosed a wide variety of textbooks on police supervision, none of which completely met our needs. We ultimately selected our text because of its general, traditional approach to the subject. A copy of the text was provided to each student, and they were expected to read the entire book during the 2-week course. Because our course curriculum was still under development when the text was selected, we were able to coordinate the curriculum with the textbook, thereby minimizing conflicts.

An ideal solution to the textbook dilemma would be a monograph produced through the coordinated efforts of the teaching staff. Using a monograph would overcome the deficiencies of a textbook and at the same time would retain the benefits of using a text.

The Students—A Profile

Some basic statistical data were collected and analyzed for five classes. A total of 111 students were in these classes, with an average class size of 22.

The method used for data collection makes the data particularly susceptible to error, and the data are not intended to represent an accurate statistical treatment. The figures do, however, shed light on the contemporary police supervisor and perhaps indicate some trends.

The average years of police experience reported by the students in the sample (N-111) was 10.4, ranging from 3 to 30 years. The typical student was an experienced police officer, but a relatively new supervisor. There were several cases of older, well-experienced firstline supervisors with 20 to 30 years on the street receiving their first exposure to formal supervisory training. The older, and generally less educated, officers experienced a greater degree of difficulty in the academic areas (reading, speaking, test taking, etc.) but performed quite admirably in practical application, leadership in a group, and decisiveness. The younger, less experienced officers also derived considerable benefit from sharing the experience of the older officers as they worked in problem-solving groups.

The course, while being designed for firstline supervisors, drew officers from a variety of police ranks. The typical class contained 1 officer above the rank of lieutenant (deputy chief, inspector, etc.), 2 lieutenants, 13 sergeants, 2 corporals, and 4 patrol officers. The patrol officers were usually upward bound and had been selected for promotion or were functioning as acting sergeants. Students come from all sizes and types of departments from all over the State, representing county, city, and university police departments.

With the influx of women into law enforcement, one would expect an increase in female students in supervisory courses. This, however, has not been our experience. Thus far, only one female officer, a patrol officer from a university department, has been enrolled in the new course.

One of our most significant findings was the level of formal education found in our sample. Seventy-three percent of the students sampled had some post high school education, 57 percent reported 2 or more years of college, 10 percent had a bachelor's degree or better, 3 percent had a master's degree or better, and one student had a law degree. These figures reflect a movement toward a better educated permanent cadre of police officers—the captains and chiefs of tomorrow.

An overwhelming majority of the supervisory students were alert, cooperative, and highly motivated. They report an increased level of confidence in their ability to perform supervisory functions following training. Students with previous supervisory experience frequently report that although they had generally been doing the "right" thing on the street, they did not understand why. Training confirmed their "gut-level" instincts and increased their confidence and ability to progress professionally.

In spite of an average tenure of 10 years, most of the officers had not become so cynical or demoralized that they were unwilling to try new ideas and innovative approaches. A common student response to modern management and supervisory theory, however, is, "I agree with the concept and I think it will work, but not in our department." Although it is by no means universal, many of the students believe their departments are stagnating and their superior officers are uninspired and unwilling to consider or try new and different management approaches. A large majority of the supervisors in our classes reflect the belief that in their departments, they are neither treated nor do they feel like they are a part of management. They believe that policy is made at higher levels and filtered down to them for implementation. A question frequently voiced by supervisory students is, "Why don't you get the captains, chiefs and sheriffs down here to teach them this material?"

Perhaps, as more trained supervisors move to higher management positions within the less progressive departments, these types of perceptions will be modified.

Conclusion

Students in our firstline supervision courses are not being presented new or different information. The information is basic, and for the most part, is traditional supervisory theory and concept. What is different is the method of delivery. Rather than the traditional lecture method of instruction, the information is being presented in a performance mode. The improvement of student response and learning in the performance-oriented course, as compared to the old method, is radical.

Although improvements in the course and its delivery will continue, the primary goal of supervisory training is, we hope, being realized. That goal is better and more efficient supervisory practices at the street level, resulting in better law enforcement.

About the Author

Jack B. Molden is a Professor, Police Training Institute, University of Illinois, Champaign, Illinois where he has trained police officers for almost twenty years. He specializes in supervision and management and in field training. He has taught, written and consulted widely in these subject areas. He holds a M.S. in Education from Kansas State College of Emporia and a B.A. in Police Science from Wichita State University. In seventeen years of active law enforcement he was Chief of Police, Emporia, Kansas, Criminal Investigator, U.S. Treasury Department, and served in a variety of jobs on the Wichita, Kansas police department. Professor Molden is a graduate of the 82nd Session of the FBI National Academy and the U.S. Treasury Enforcement Officers School. Molden has published over forty articles in professional law enforcement journals and is a columnist for Law and Order Magazine *where he authors "Training Officer's Notes."*

CHAPTER III
EVALUATING

INTRODUCTION TO CHAPTER III:
Evaluating

After recruiting and training personnel, departments must evaluate what those people actually do and how well they do it. To make such determinations, departments must depend on good personnel and program evaluation systems.

Article 10, by Edwin L. Moreau, provides guidance for one of the toughest interviews law enforcement officers perform: The performance appraisal interview. Letting police personnel know how they are doing can be an effective and a constructive process if approached strategically. The author includes 5 basic questions and outlines the steps for a good interview.

In Article 11, Hillary M. Robinette focuses on a particular police problem: The Problem Employee. This article focuses directly on the problem employee, looks at a nationwide survey concerning marginal performers, and offers some concrete suggestions for dealing with the problem employee.

Article 12 looks at evaluating the programs of any department. In an era of doing more with less, evaluating the accomplishments of personnel is essential. Richard C. Sonnichsen and Gustave A. Schick argue that program evaluation can help managers make better decisions and reduce uncertainty about programs and personnel by providing timely and valuable information. The authors use the FBI's evaluation program as a model and provide information on how to establish an effective and efficient office of program evaluation and how to tell if it is working well.

The Performance Appraisal Interview

By Edwin L. Moreau

Performance evaluations have prevailed since the time one man began working for another. While these evaluations have developed just recently into written, structured documents, questions pertaining to an employee's job performance have always been asked. How is the employee doing? Could this employee do more? What are his career goals? What can we do to make this employee perform better? These questions, spoken and unspoken, are presented daily and are actually performance evaluations.

Although structured performance appraisals have been used by private industry and law enforcement since the 1960's, it wasn't until the early 1970's that these evaluations became the basis for determining merit increases, promotions, transfers, and decisionmaking.[1] Early evaluations complied with the growth of American industry and the managerial motivation theories that abounded at the time. Managers looked at Abraham Maslow's Hierarchy-of-Needs Theory and set forth evaluation systems to determine where their employees placed on the hierarchy, where they were going, and how the satisfaction of these needs were actually affecting employee performance. Evaluations also tested the employees' performance against the Motivation-Hygiene Theory of Frederick Herzberg.

Managers quickly realized that structured performance evaluations were excellent for documenting their decisionmaking activities. As labor became more organized, managers were forced to "show cause" for their various personnel decisions, e.g., raises, denials of raises, promotions, denials of promotions, requests for additional personnel, transfers, etc. Almost every decision made by management could be supported by a reliable performance appraisal system.

As performance evaluation systems evolved, they took many forms. Basically, two forms are currently used by managers. With the structured, written form, the employee is evaluated toward set standards, criteria, and goals concerning the job assignment. In the second part, the supervisor/employee evaluation interview, the employee is made aware of how the supervisor perceives his job performance. The supervisor discusses the written evaluation with the employee and provides feedback on how the employee is doing in his present position. This is also a time for feedback to the supervisor of the employee's feelings, desires, goals, and fulfilled and unfilled job expectations. This evaluation interview is one of the main supervisory tools available to management today. It can be a rewarding experience for both the employee and supervisor.

Preparation

The employee performance appraisal interview is usually not one of the duties a supervisor looks forward to, unless he is fortunate to manage only high-quality performers as employees. Unfortunately, there are few supervisors in law enforcement or business who enjoy this luxury, and these are normally supervisors of "special" units who have had the opportunity to hand pick their subordinates. Most supervisors have a mixture of high, marginal, and low performers. Interview sessions involving marginal and low performers can be very disconcerting and stressful to the supervisor. Douglas McGregor once said that supervisors have "a normal dislike of having to criticize an employee."[2] Additionally, a supervisor, like anyone else, does not like to hear uncomplimentary remarks about himself and his unit, which frequently is the case in interviews with low performers as their defensive mechanisms are set in gear to combat the supervisor's criticism of their job performance.

61

Even though the appraisal may present unpleasant moments for the supervisor and employee alike, it is an extremely important tool. One bad interview can destroy a favorable relationship that has existed for some time and quite possibly set an unfavorable climate for the future. However, one good interview can establish a relationship of mutual trust and understanding that could carry on forever.

The appraisal interview presents a unique opportunity for two-way communication at that particular level of the organization. It is an opportunity to recognize the quality performance of an exceptional employee. Likewise, it is an opportunity to assist or coach the marginal- or low-performance employee to improve job performance. To some supervisors or managers, the appraisal interview is "forced" communication, and they have strong feelings against such circumstances. However, other than the cursory communication in the hall, locker room, or line-up room, many supervisors communicate very little with their employees, and this forced communication is often better than none at all.

The appraisal interview could possibly be one of the most important training sessions an employee or supervisor, in some cases, has during the year. There is actual one-on-one, face-to-face dialogue between the instructor (supervisor) and the student (employee). This would be considered the ultimate training session by any instructor or student. For the period of time the two are together, they have each other's undivided attention. There is no sharing of each other's time with third-party problems. The "instruction" can proceed at the pace of the employee, not, as in classroom settings, as slow as the slowest student or as fast as the sharpest student. As an instructor for over 15 years, I have yet to encounter this opportunity outside the interview setting.

Handled properly, the appraisal interview can provide several advantages for the employee, the supervisor, and the organization. The interview provides personal feedback to the employee. Personal feedback has almost universally proved to have a strong relationship to job satisfaction and productivity. The interview can provide the employee a broader understanding of why and how he needs to modify work behavior or performance to improve both personal and organizational effec-

tiveness. The interview can instill self-confidence in the employee, as well as more confidence or trust in the supervisor and the supervisor's actions. This self-confidence can lead to greater creativity by the employee which, in turn, leads to greater creativity in problem solving for the organization because of increased employee input. A cooperative climate develops which increases individual and subsequently group motivation toward achieving performance and organizational goals. Increased employee self-confidence and self-reliance improve as an employee develops the ability to recognize problems and act upon them without additional supervisory assistance. This allows the supervisor to concentrate on other management functions and activities. The sum of these positive effects results in less supervisory reluctance to discuss problems and possible solutions to these problems with the employees.

Another possible benefit of properly conducted interviews is that reports of these interviews provide documentation for the reasons behind many of the supervisor's decisions. The transfer of personnel is often linked directly to the evaluation interview where managers attempt to work with employees in formulating career paths. After a positive exchange between the supervisor and employee, often new or self-enriching assignments are needed to motivate an employee. The appraisal interview and its subsequent documentation will support the move.

Additionally, with the growth of a breed of questioning, rights-conscious workers, organizations and managers can expect to be challenged in their decisions. The performance appraisal documentation is being introduced increasingly into court proceedings to combat discrimination claims. Assignments, attitudes, and performance records agreed on by both management and the employee are often prima facie evidence of fair employment practices.[3]

Before getting into a discussion of the interview itself, there are several areas which a supervisor/manager must fully understand in order to make the interview worthwhile. Perhaps the most basic is understanding and subsequently avoiding the several obstacles which stand in the way of a rewarding interview.

Failure to accept a subordinate as a person can ruin a supervisor or manager. The supervisor/manager must realize that regardless of the position held, the employee has individual opinions and ideas. These ideas should be listened to, accepted, and considered. Whether they are useful or constructive, it is important that the employee have the opportunity to express them. Additionally, each employee has prejudices, likes and dislikes, and fears. By understanding these, the astute manager can improve the working environment, thus improving the chance of increased performance.

Not to be contradictory, the supervisor must also not be overly concerned with why a subordinate acts the way he does, rather he (the supervisor) must seek answers for improving the employee's performance.

A supervisor/manager often falls into the trap of playing amateur psychologist by trying to label employees into certain categories. Examples of this are tagging employees with "bad attitudes," "hot tempers," or "poor self-image." Since most managers do not have the background to make such prognostications, they fall into the trap of trying to treat the "illness" without having fully diagnosed the disease. Labeling an employee and subsequently treating the disease can lead to a form of self-fulfilling prophecy on the part of the employee. His exposure to the manager's cure can give him the disease.

Once a supervisor understands that the employee is a person with individual beliefs and feelings, it is the supervisor/manager's responsibility to develop listening and interviewing techniques to determine an employee's problems without developing the appearance of prying. The feeling of having someone peer into your personal life is one of the great turnoffs for most people. Open, responsive communication can bring out this information without inducing the feeling of prying.

The final obstacle is that of using the interview to punish the employee. The interview is to be a fact-finding, information-sharing, problem-solving intercourse, not a place for disciplinary actions. Once the criteria are set, discussed fully, and agreed upon, the failures can be dealt with later. If the employee believes he is going to the interview to be reprimanded, he will begin to set his defensive mechanisms in order and the interview will be worthless, as it will be with either a one-way conversation or a two-way shouting match.[4]

The Interview

The interview itself, as previously mentioned, is one of the most important actions of a supervisor/manager. The atmosphere/setting must be structured to ensure everything is covered correctly and in a positive manner; yet, not so structured as to stifle the employee's input. Three activities should be done by the supervisor prior to the interview.

First, the supervisor/manager should notify the employee of the upcoming interview, designating both the time and location. Advance notification gives the employee time to make any necessary changes in his schedule, as well as any personal adjustments (haircuts, clean brass, polish shoes, etc.). The employee also should be given copies of the interview form or the job classification/criteria of his particular duties. Most departments issue the above material to all personnel so the notification may simply refer to the specific sections of the material upon which the appraisal is being based. Providing the employee with advance notification and information will help reduce anxiety about the interview.

Second, the supervisor should select a proper location for the interview. A location free of telephone and visitor interruptions conveys a feeling of importance to the employee. A "neutral ground" concept is preferred. A conference room, a small library room, or a third person's office fits this concept ideally. The supervisor should avoid using the employee's office since he can be distracted easily by unfinished work, family pictures, etc. In turn, the supervisor's office is often considered "holy ground" by employees and can present a sense of awe. Additionally, any display of personal awards, diplomas, pictures of high officials, etc., could emit a sense of power or superiority.

Third, the supervisor should select the proper time for the interview. There is no hard and set rule as to the length of the interview, as there are too many variables. However, a proper appraisal interview should take at least an hour. It is also recommended that the interview be set for early in the work day when both the supervisor and employee are fresh and alert and have yet to become involved in the business of the day.

The interview is best started with a short period of informal conversation. This unstructured period will help dissipate feelings of anxiety and apprehensiveness usually experienced by both the employee and supervisor. Besides placing both at ease, this procedure often encourages normally quiet or reserved persons to express themselves and their thoughts.

Once the employee is at ease, the formal appraisal interview can begin. There are five basic questions which will be at the heart of the interview, although they are probably not officially stated by either the employee or supervisor.

1) "How am I doing?"

2) "What am I doing right?"

3) "Where do I need to improve?"

4) "What can be done to help me do my job better?"

5) "Where do I want to go from here, and what should be done to prepare me for it?"

The answers to these five basic questions should be included in practically every point discussed on the evaluation form.[5]

The employee should have a blank copy of the evaluation form, while the supervisor should have a copy completed in pencil, since it is subject to change after discussion of each evaluation factor with the employee. This is not to be viewed as saying every factor is subject to change depending upon the persuasiveness of the employee. Rather, it indicates the possibility of modification or adjustment on the part of the manager. If the manager exhibits inflexibility, then the employee thinks "what's the use" and does not communicate his feelings. However, if the supervisor is willing to listen, it gives the employee the opportunity to influence the evaluation. It gives him the chance to offer personal ideas for improvement. It also provides the employee an opportunity to enlighten the supervisor on activities he possibly missed or misunderstood.[6]

As the employee will be evaluated against a set of standards for each evaluation factor, it is important that the standards be written and made available to personnel. For each activity or task performed and thus evaluated by the supervisor/manager, there must be a standard, an acceptable quantitative or qualitative level of performance. These standards must be made available to the employee early in his assignment to the position. The employee must understand the standards thoroughly in order to satisfactorily perform the work or task. Therefore, great care should be taken in formulating, working, and communicating these standards. Presently, many departments through the use of task forces or other participatory management actions get the employees themselves involved in formulating performance standards. In fact, one of the offshoots of the appraisal interview is the redesigning of standards which are found to be questionable, unclear, restrictive, or too liberal for effective measurement. A very effective tool in this process is to seek the employee's definition of standards with which he seems to be having problems. It would possibly not affect the current evaluation, but could assist with the future performance if only because the employee had some input into the formulation of the new standard.

Another important factor of the appraisal form will be the rating scale for each performance factor evaluated. Again, precise definitions of each rating should be published and be familiar to the employee. An important tool is having the employee define each rating in his own words prior to discussing the performance factors. This description and the discussion that follows as to the supervisor's definition of each rating places both parties on "common" ground. Once both parties agree to the meaning of each rating, then there is little room for argument once the facts are presented. In many rating systems, documentation is required for rates outside the satisfactory ranges, both high and low. The interview phase will bring out "verbal" documentation for each rating, and therefore, let an employee understand the particular rating for each factor evaluated.

Often, supervisors will rate employees in the satisfactory ranges to avoid having to document reasons for a particular rating. During the appraisal interview, however, the supervisor and employee discuss the rating of each factor. Because he will have to document "verbally" each rating, a supervisor will give a more complete or honest evaluation. He cannot hide laziness or disinterest in the evaluation by staying in the satisfactory (or undocumented) level since he will be questioned by the employee on the ratings of all performance factors.

Once the standards are fully understood and the rating scale for each factor is agreed upon by both parties, the interview can formally begin. It is recommended that the supervisor initially read the performance factor and then ask the employee to rate himself verbally, giving reasons for the rating. One often finds that employees rate themselves lower than the supervisor in almost every factor when given a chance. Once the employee finishes his dialogue concerning the rating, the supervisor then advises him of the actual rating, documenting the reasons "verbally." If the supervisory rating is higher, the employee is relieved and often surprised and begins to develop confidence in the supervisor's "good judgment." Of course, there is usually very little discussion on the part of the employee for a change in the rating. In instances of higher employee self-rating than supervisory rating, the situation is usually reversed. Employees may attempt to persuade the supervisor to change the rating or may lose confidence in the supervisor's judgment. This situation brings about the key to a good interview, which is "the ability to involve the interviewee in two-way communication." This is a prerequisite for acceptance of the evaluation and therefore establishment of goals for the future.[7]

Since the goals of the appraisal interview are to let the employee know his efforts are recognized and appreciated, to inspire the employee to improve his performance, and to discuss the quality of his performance,[8] the dialogue over disagreeing ratings is important. Since the participants have previously reached "common" ground on the value of each rating, the facts or details can now be brought out. There are often pitfalls to both sides of the discussion. Supervisors and employees alike often take into consideration the time frame of the evaluation. Often, prior history or previous personal feelings are involved. Additionally, recent history (last week or two) is considered and thus can confuse or corrupt the validity of the evaluation. This discussion can bring both parties back into line.

Other factors can also cloud the issue. Supervisors may not be aware of all the activities of the employee. Often "good" jobs are not brought to his attention as regularly as the "screw-ups," and the dialogue will bring these to the surface. The

supervisor could possibly have his own ideas about the performance of certain tasks and can suggest activities which would improve the performance of the "unknowing" employee. The interview can "sell" the employee on the idea that he could improve after all.

The supervisor assumes two roles in the appraisal interview, the judge and the coach. The role of the judge should be down played, although it is important. As judge, the supervisor must make decisions concerning the results of the employee's work, measuring the results against the set standards. As judge, however, the supervisor must remember to be fair and impartial in his personal feelings about the employee and keep both the goals of the organization and future of the employee in mind. The supervisor, as judge, must remember the results of a study conducted in private industry that pointed out the effects of criticism in an evaluation:

1) Criticism has a negative effect on achievement of goals.
2) Criticism sets up a defensive state in the employee and thus produces inferior performance.[9]

The second role, that of coach or counselor, is the most important in the interview process. As ratings are discussed for individual performance factors, the coach can assist the employee in setting goals for improvement. He can offer suggestions for avenues in obtaining those goals and point out weaknesses which interfere with attaining them. Praise for the employee has short term effects, lasting only as long as the interview. However, the employee will remember the criticism long after the interview has ended. Telling an employee his good or superior points helps ease the impact of inferior points.

The role of the coach is very important to setting goals. Allowing the employee the opportunity to participate in determining his goals and the goals of the department is critical for today's managers who have to confront problems which become more complex with each passing day. Employee input often provides the feedback needed to combat this complexity. Not using employee input and suggestions would be tantamount to having a research staff and not using the fruits of their efforts. Employees should be encouraged by supervisors to offer suggestions for improvement, weigh alternatives, and make recommendations. Participation by the employee in the goal-setting procedure improves job performance which, in turn, results in improved organizational operations.[10]

After listing the factors separately with the individual ratings, the supervisor would provide a composite rating of how the employee is doing overall. Any comparison with other employees should be avoided. The employee should be evaluated only against the set standards. The supervisor should again point out the strong and weak areas of the evaluation and reiterate the goals and the avenues to obtain them that were mutually set. He should then ask for any final comments or suggestions concerning the evaluation or interview.

As soon as possible, the completed evaluation form should be provided to the employee with comments, suggestions, and goals documented. The employee should also have an avenue for appeal if he believes the evaluation is unfair.

Followup after the interview is equally important, since several comments and suggestions may arise which should be reported back to the employee. This followup can be provided through a formal memorandum or a set meeting by informal conversation with the employee. It will determine whether the goals and needs of the department and employee are being met and ensure that the employee is attempting to obtain mutually agreed on goals. Followup also gives clues as to the effectiveness of the interview, as well as demonstrates to the employee that the supervisor is seriously considering his recommendations and suggestions.

Summary

Only recently has management begun to use the appraisal interview to its fullest benefit. It is still looked upon unfavorably by many supervisors and employees, but it can be a very useful tool for supervision. The interview, when properly conducted, can present face-to-face discussion between the employee and supervisor. This discussion provides an opportunity to compliment the employee for his contributions to the job and organization as well as point out his shortcomings. In addition, the interview is a time for coaching/counseling the employee on methods for improvement, as well as setting future goals for both the employee and the organization.

The performance appraisal interview presents an opportunity for the supervisor to enhance self-esteem in the employee, to establish a good work relationship and a foundation for a better work environment, and to increase productivity through increased job satisfaction and participation in decisionmaking functions. In addition, followup procedures to the appraisal interview show the employee that his supervisor is interested in his input into the affairs of the department. These procedures also provide feedback as to the effectiveness of the interview and the attainment of individual and organizational goals. The properly conducted appraisal interview is one of the most valuable management tools available today.

About the Author

Ed Moreau is a Captain with the Winston-Salem, North Carolina, Police Department. Since joining the department in 1968, he advanced through the ranks, obtaining the rank of Captain in 1980. Ed has served in several capacities in the Winston-Salem Police Department, from patrol to training, and is currently the Commander of the Criminal Investigations Division.

He holds a Bachelor of Science Degree from Guilford College, with a major in Administration of Justice. Ed also instructs law enforcement courses at several community colleges.

Footnotes

[1] Cal W. Downs, G. Paul Smeyak, and Ernest Martin, *Professional Interviewing* (New York, N.Y.: Harper and Row, 1980), p. 161.

[2] Paul R. Timm, *Managerial Communication: A Finger on the Pulse* (Englewood Cliffs, N.J.: Prentice-Hall, Inc., 1980), p. 163.

[3] DeVries, Morrison, Shullman, and Gerlach, *Performance Appraisal on the Line* (New York, N.Y.: John Wiley and Sons, Inc., 1981), p. 15.

4 Supra note 2.

5 *State of Maine Employee Handbook*, 1978, pp. 36-39.

6 J.R. Gibb, *Leadership and Interpersonal Behavior* (New York, N.Y.: Holt, Rinehart and Winston, Inc., 1961), pp. 66-81.

7 James M. Lahiff, "Interviewing for Results," *Readings in Interpersonal and Organizational Communication* (Boston, Mass.: Allyn and Bacon, Inc., 1977), p. 405.

8 Ibid, p. 404.

9 H.H. Meyer, Emanuel Kay, J.R.P. French, Jr. , "Split Roles in Performance Appraisal," *Readings in Interpersonal and Organizational Communication* (Boston, Mass.: Allyn and Bacon, Inc., 1977), p. 339.

10 Ibid.

The Police Problem Employee

By Hillary M. Robinette

Police supervisors at all levels are concerned with the marginal and unsatisfactory police employee. They analyze causes and symptoms in an effort to understand and to solve the complex problems of job disaffection, dissatisfaction, contraorganizational behavior, and reduced performance.

With steady increases of cost-push inflation[1] and the attendant effects on the costs of recruiting, selection, and training, police managers are looking more closely at ways to improve the performance of current employees. Those officers and police employees who are judged marginal or unsatisfactory are coming under closer scrutiny by police managers for several reasons. Efforts are being directed at finding the causes of marginal performance and in determining solutions to the problem.

This article explores the issue of the marginal performer in the police department and the changing environments in today's society that have created different employee expectations, and therefore, disaffection and marginal performance. As part of this examination, the article also considers the results of a 1981 survey of police managers' perceptions of employee performance and offers some suggestions for dealing with marginal performance.

The Clay-Yates Study

The results of a research study conducted by Special Agents Reginald R. Clay and Robert E. Yates of the FBI Academy indicated the scope of the problem of marginal police performers. The researchers set out to identify and profile the police marginal and unsatisfactory employee by using a questionnaire survey given to a nationwide sample of police supervisors and managers.[2]

The Clay-Yates study was completed in early 1981. One hundred and eighty-three randomly selected participants of the 117th Session of the FBI National Academy responded to an initial survey

instrument. The instrument was modified for validation and then given to an additional 1,200 law enforcement supervisors. Five hundred and fifty-three of these were used to derive a significant sample of data for consideration.[3]

The study respondents were all supervisors of law enforcement personnel. Ninety-seven percent of the respondents had been police supervisors for over 2 years; 93 percent had been in police work for 7 or more years. The respondent group represented a variety of departments and agencies: 16 percent were from departments of 1,000 or more sworn personnel; 54 percent were from departments of intermediate size; and 30 percent were from small departments (50 or fewer sworn personnel). (See fig. 1.)

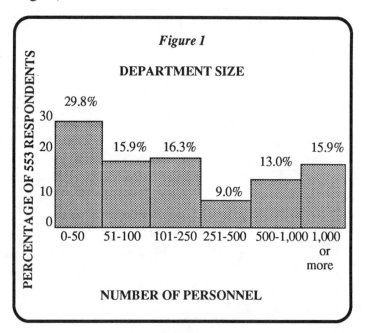

Figure 1

DEPARTMENT SIZE

The researchers set out to identify employee problem areas by frequency of occurrence and severity of the problem. Those surveyed were given 16 choices of problem behavior and asked to select the most frequently occurring and the most serious. The responses indicated that the most frequent employee problem area is often viewed as the most serious; 38.5 percent cited the most frequently occurring problem was the police officer who did "just enough to get by." The data also indicated that the supervisors regarded this employee as their most serious problem. The second most frequently occurring problem was absenteeism and tardiness (19.9 percent) followed by resistance to change (11.2 percent). (See figs. 2 & 3.)

Police Problem Employee Profile

An examination of the Clay-Yates data produces a profile of the police problem employee in the United States today. The problem employee is a male officer assigned to patrol or investigation who has some college education and is between 25 and

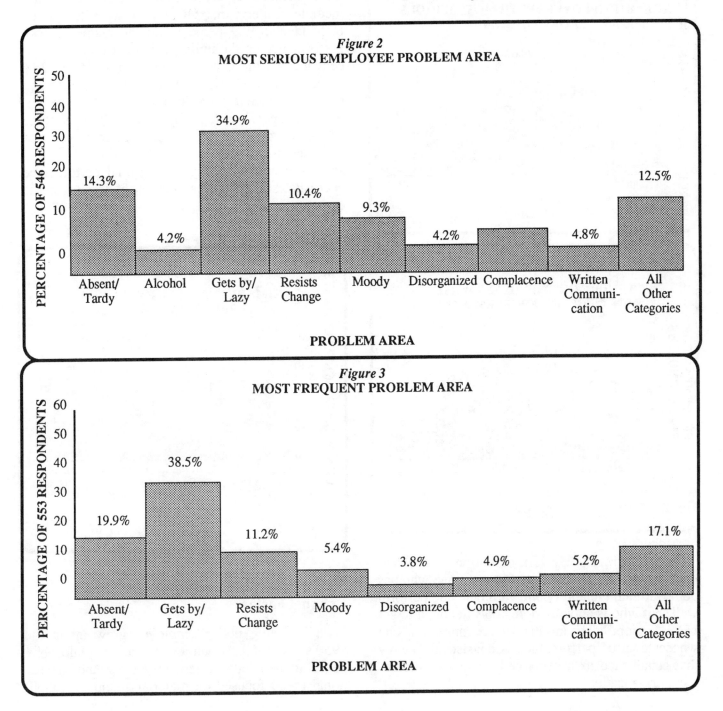

Figure 2
MOST SERIOUS EMPLOYEE PROBLEM AREA

Figure 3
MOST FREQUENT PROBLEM AREA

39 years of age. As stated before, the most frequent and most serious difficulty is that he does only enough work to get by. The study shows that the largest single group of these employees (28 percent) were 30 to 34 years of age and had 6 to 10 years' service with the department. (See figs. 4 & 5.)

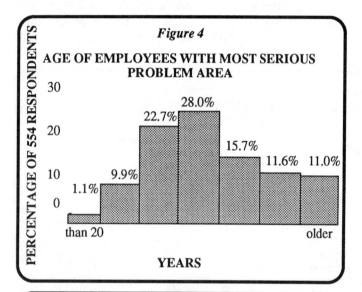

Figure 4

AGE OF EMPLOYEES WITH MOST SERIOUS PROBLEM AREA

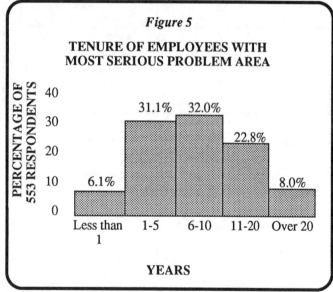

Figure 5

TENURE OF EMPLOYEES WITH MOST SERIOUS PROBLEM AREA

Implied in the study is a definition of problem employees. The marginal performer is one who has demonstrated the ability and willingness to perform well, but who is actually doing only "enough to get by on the job."[4] The unsatisfactory employee is one whose level of performance is consistently below that established as acceptable by the law enforcement organization.

In addition, the Clay-Yates study asked police supervisors who were managing problem employees to identify the causes of the problems. Although complex by nature, these causes of poor performance can be broadly assigned as follows: (a) external influences, i.e., factors away from the job environment, (b) the personal and unique weaknesses of the individual, (c) departmental mismanagement, i.e., organizational forces other than the immediate supervisor, and finally, (d) the immediate supervisor. Of the Clay-Yates study respondents, 39.9 percent laid the blame of poor performance on the individual employee; 26.9 percent located the cause in outside influences; 26.6 percent accused departmental mismanagement; only 6.6 percent fixed responsibility on the immediate supervisor. (See fig. 6.) In 60 percent of the cases, the duration of marginal performance had extended over a year.[5]

A clear understanding of marginal performance necessitates a closer examination of some of these causes.

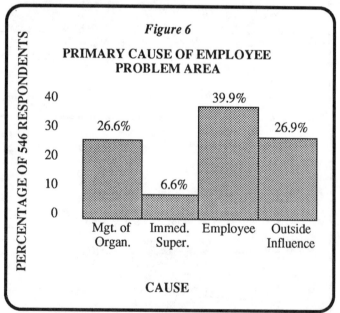

Figure 6

PRIMARY CAUSE OF EMPLOYEE PROBLEM AREA

External Factors

Today's young police employee grew up in the 1950's and 1960's when a personalistic philosophy began to permeate American society and the national mood focused on material abundance, GNP growth, and technological advancement. American workers began to change the kind of jobs they performed. In the 1950's, 65 percent of the work force was engaged in industrial occupations and only about 17 percent was employed in information (personal service) occupations. In the following 30 years, the number of Americans in industry dropped to 27 percent while the ranks of the "white-collar" information worker rose to 58 percent in 1980.[6]

During the 1970's, a "self-fulfillment" movement started to spread throughout the United States. By the late 1970's, national surveys showed more than 7 out of 10 Americans (72 percent) spent a great deal of time thinking about themselves and their inner lives.[7] Traditional values were completely reversed, and the self-denial ethic which once fueled the faltering engines of industry was lost in the search for self-fulfillment.

The rising expectations of an expanding middle class and the higher educational levels of those entering the work force combined to produce a perception of needed self-fulfillment. Police departments were not excepted. During this time, the U.S. President's Commission on Law Enforcement and Administration of Justice called for the professionalization of police. The U.S. Congress voted large Federal appropriations to increase police officer education and management training.[8] With subsequent liberal LEAA educational funds, law enforcement and criminal justice programs proliferated in newly created junior colleges and technical schools, as well as on traditional campuses. Previously, such programs were not available to the police aspirant. Education raises personal expectations. Those entering the police profession during the 1960's and 1970's brought expectations of advancement and personal income growth which traditional police departments can scarcely meet. Such a reality is bound to cause individual frustration and other discontent manifested in "burn out" and other forms of counter-productive behavior.

The police "problem employee" of the 1980's comes from that social, economic, and psychological turmoil. The pervading cultural psychology of affluence has reversed the self-denial ethic; the tradition of police service to the community is, in some instances, also reversed. Those who entered police service seeking affluence and self-fulfillment become bored with routines and cynical toward the public after the excitement of mastering police skills is gone.

Traditional police organization structures leave very little room at the top for large numbers of educated recruits. In 1977, 42 percent of the officers of departments surveyed by the Police Executive Research Forum had associate or higher degrees.[9]

The officers came to police work with expectations of promotion, pay increases, and enlarging job responsibilities. Not all of the expectations can be met. Frustration occurs, enthusiasm for the job diminishes, and behavior changes, often for the worse. Moreover, many of the young recruits joining departments today bring with them a psychology of affluence which moves them to seek increasing salary levels. This attitude flies in the harsh face of economics. Cost-push inflation and antitax movements, such as Proposition 13 in California and Proposition 2.5 in Massachusetts, combine to strain public revenue. Cutback Federal and State budget management requires police to share smaller and smaller portions of public revenues. Budget cuts affect salary levels. Consequently, there is less to go around at a time when individual expectations of affluence are rising. Such countervailing forces are another source of frustration for the individual officer.

Time-Psych Zones and the Expectation Curve

Coupled with social change are the individual, physical, and mental developments of each person's life. These circumstances of personal change can be described as "time-psych zones." Daniel L. Levinson published the results of a study of basic importance in his book, *The Seasons of a Man's Life*.[10] It is the first such study which explains adult development according to an age-linked timetable. He relates each stage of development to a man's job as the primary base for his life in society. The findings indicate that as we grow older, motivation patterns change. Personal, physical, and environmental circumstances change. Needs change; therefore, behavior changes.

Time-psych zones are the zones of personal expectations which change with age. In early adulthood, during one's first major job responsibility, achievement expectations run strong and high. These are modified by experience and reality during the midlife transition and become settled only through the turbulence of the transition. Often, this transition is marked by confusion of needs and desires. The desire to acquire additional possessions, to taste life in the fast lane, to travel to new places, and to meet new and important people engaged in exciting activities are all seen as needs. Personal goals are shaped by the marketing media which also raises these expectations in order to increase product sales. The individual needs more money, more leisure, and more freedom from commitment to job and home. As Yankelovich claims, "... desires are infinite. Anyone trapped in the fallacy that the self is a failure to the extent that all one's desires are not satisfied has set herself or himself up for frustration."[11] Stability is regained during the middle-adult era and carries over through a less turbulent transition into late adulthood. The significance and effect of the stages and transition on a police officer's career and worklife are important.

The early stages of a police officer's career are usually characterized by high expectations of service achievement. He often daydreams of exciting successes in his assignment. He views the successes as necessary coin with which to buy preferment and career-enhancing assignments of increased responsibility. Persons riding the expectation curve in their 20's and early 30's are adaptive to change. They view change as challenging, presenting new opportunities for achievement. They have a high tolerance for negative hygiene factors in the work environment and conditions.[12] They are future-oriented, seldom reflective, and have a high readiness for training. They have a low tolerance for perceived opportunity restriction. Often, they equate self-fulfillment with career advancement and will consider any real or imagined attempt to restrict their advancement with animosity and resistance.

As officers peak on the expectation curve (usually during or just after Levinson's midlife transition), they adjust their expectations. Motivation patterns and other job performance characteristics change. Those on this flat downside of the expectation curve are resistant to change. They often view a change in tactics, procedures, or policy as a threat

to their new-found stability and will actively resist change, or worse, try to subvert it. The old saying about "not being able to teach an old dog new tricks" applies some folk wisdom to the reality. These officers also have a low tolerance for hygiene negatives and can take personal offense at minor adjustments in their work environments. They respond negatively to any deterioration in perks or seniority and working conditions. They are present-oriented and think of success in terms of completing today's task and not in terms of tomorrow's assignment. They have a high tolerance for stable policies, rules, and procedures and a low readiness for training, new job-learning experiences, and additional career-related formal education. (See fig. 7.)

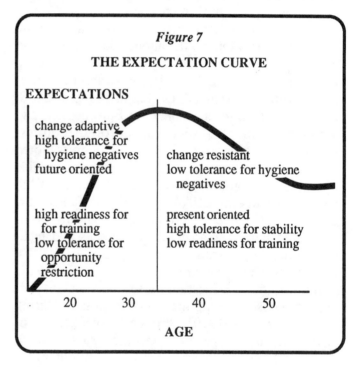

Figure 7

THE EXPECTATION CURVE

The results of the Clay-Yates study support this expectation curve phenomenon. The large majority of marginal police performers fall in this age group. As reflected in the data, the average marginal performer has between 8 and 16 years' police service.

Change Comes to the Police Department

Changes in the social environment, values, demographics, technology, and economy have all combined to create a managerial atmosphere of turbulence. Once the most stable of municipal organizations, police departments now struggle through strikes, reorganizations, new public policy, and vastly increased operating costs. Between 1967 and 1977, the per capita cost of policing in a large city had risen from $27.31 to over $91, an increase of over 257 percent.[13]

Police work is labor-intensive. The human resources are the most effective of the resources applied in policing and also the most costly. Any cost-reduction analysis or efficiency-improvement effort must focus on improving human resource management. The intuitive perception of this reality has generated concerned interest in the management and salvage of the marginal performer.

The marginal or unsatisfactory performer is costly to police organizations. The difficult work of solving the problem of the marginal employee is discomforting to police managers. Some say it is impossible to take effective action because of legal restraints or union policies. Others cite lack of training in managerial skills for shift supervisors and first-line commanders. All are uncomfortable when confronted with the problem employee. Uncomfortable or not, however, police managers must seek solutions.

The Management Challenge

If these data and the trends they suggest are accurately understood, they raise new challenges for police managers. The first is to analyze carefully the factors which contribute to marginal police performance; the second is to find ways to keep the job alive for those who once did it well and with enthusiasm but who have now lost their motivation. Finally, police managers must develop and use effective coaching and documentation skills.

The first challenge, which is analytical in nature, is the most difficult. The police manager is action-oriented. He thrives in an atmosphere of activity. He has little time, inclination, or training for thoughtful reflection. George Odiorne identifies this predisposition as an "activity trap." He writes:

"The activity trap is a self-feeding mechanism if you do not turn it around. Everybody becomes attached to some irrelevancy and does his or her job too well. Its ultimate stage is when the [chief] himself loses sight of why the [department] exists, and demands more and more activity rather than results. . . .

"Meanwhile, all this activity eats up resources, money, space, budgets, savings, and human energy like a mammoth tape worm.

"While it is apparent that the activity trap . . . fails to achieve missions, it has an equally dangerous side-effect on people; they *shrink* personally and professionally."[14]

Without constant attention to the results and contributions that a police manager expects of his subordinates, the manager falls into the activity trap. Some of his subordinates will shrink into the rote process of a job and lose sight of its goals and objectives. With the sure knowledge that activity without goals is wasteful, it is no surprise that these officers become bored or dissatisfied.

As Odiorne points out, however, the trap is not inevitable. It can be resisted and circumvented by enlightened and analytical leadership. The challenge of supervisory analysis calls for the police manager to focus on results in directing his subordinates, then clarify and communicate the results to the people doing the work. Only then will the work itself produce the satisfaction and enthusiasm that keeps the police employee productive. This is not an easy task, but it is specifically managerial and executive in nature. Where the symptoms of marginal performance are unenthusiastic and dissatisfied officers, the manager would do well to find out whether looking busy has become safer than being productive.

The next challenge is finding ways to energize employees. With clear goals and objectives identified, how does the police manager secure employee commitment and enthusiasm for task accomplishment?

The answer here lies in the manager's own commitment and enthusiasm. He must avoid the danger of transparent management, which is the depersonalized processing of organizational directives. If he becomes an executive rubber stamp, he will be viewed as an empty suit, not an effective police manager.

The third challenge is that of developing one's own perception, understanding, and communication skills. To meet this challenge, the police manager must examine his own assumptions about the marginal performer. He must test those assumptions against his wider and probably more objective nonorganizational experiences. He must learn to be sensitive to the expectations of his subordinates. He must also keep in touch with his own time-psych zones. More attention is now directed at officers and employees who are not meeting standards.

Daniel J. Bell, writing in *The Police Chief,* verbalizes the interest when he says: "...there needs to be a concentration of effort to move the 'drone' type police officer into other careers outside the police profession."[15] Who is the "drone-type police officer" Bell refers to? Can causes of poor performance be identified and how can they be remedied?

A decision for dismissal or a decision for salvage with the required coaching an counseling must be made. Salvage and renewal are practical, cost-effective ways to meet the challenge. Six out of 10 police managers (65.2 percent) of those surveyed recommend that the marginal police employee be salvaged.[16]

Dismissal is difficult and impossible without documentation. Changes in the legal environment, especially those brought on by affirmative action, equal employment opportunity, and the women's movement require job analyses and validated performance standards. Job analysis and validation were activities that were formerly not required of the police. Standards are determined and stated. Formal defense of standards and associated personnel actions are now required, if not in a court of law then in an appeals commission or grievance board.

Strangely, the procedures to support either a dismissal or salvage decision are similar. Effective coaching *and* a permanent, legal termination begin with documentation. The manger must begin with a clear concept of the unit's goals and objectives. These must be communicated to the employee clearly. The work the employee is expected to do must relate directly to the goals and objectives and be so explained to the employee. The manager is required to plan carefully the marginal subordinate's work, just as the subordinate is required to perform the work. Some measurement of progress must be agreed upon. Performance must be documented on a timely basis; appraisal must be regular, realistic, and frequent.

Performance appraisal is just that—an evaluation of actual performance. The police manager needs to pay personal and honest attention to the work the marginal performer does and the work he fails to do. Only then can both understand when the work is done and the objectives are achieved. The manager has the opportunity to reinforce behavior in a nondestructive and objective way. The manager's feedback is the employee's guide to improving performance.

Significantly, almost half of the supervisors polled in the Clay-Yates study (44.5 percent) claimed success in dealing with their problem employees. The probability of success is good, but success is the result of difficult managerial work.

In these times of shrinking resources, police managers are looking for ways to do more with less—ways to meet the rising public demand to reduce violent crime, restore peace and tranquility, and spend fewer public dollars. There is no room for continued marginal performance in police work. Success can be obtained by a recommitment to excellence by the police manager, by a sensitive and attentive concern for the officers under his leadership, and by the acquisition and development of managerial skills.

About the Author

Hillary M. Robinette is a Supervisory Special Agent of the Federal Bureau of Investigation. A 17-year veteran of the Bureau, he is currently assigned to the Management Science Unit of the FBI Academy at Quantico, Virginia. He teaches courses in management and supervision to the FBI National Academy with special interest in police first-line supervisory problems. He is an Adjunct Instructor of the University of Virginia. He reported to his present assignment after 11 years of investigative work as an FBI Special Agent in Texas and Ohio, and he lives in Prince William County, Virginia, near the town of Dumfries.

His articles on management and training have appeared in various law enforcement journals and publications. He has traveled to police departments throughout the nation to present training programs in Managing Marginal Performance. He has been a Visiting Lecturer at the Canadian Police College in Ottawa, Canada, and a member of the directing staff at the Police Staff College in Bramshill, England.

Upon completion of undergraduate studies at St. Joseph's University in Philadelphia, Pennsylvania, he served as a line officer in the U.S. Navy. He holds an MBA degree from the University of Dayton.

Footnotes

[1] The term "cost-push inflation" is used to describe the inflationary spiral in which increasing costs act to push up prices and wages in a cyclical effect.

[2] *Problem Employee Survey: An Analysis of Employee Problem Areas in Law Enforcement*, Reginald R. Clay and Robert E. Yates, FBI Academy, Quantico, Va., 1981, p. 3.

[3] "Of the 1,200 law enforcement supervisors surveyed, questionnaire responses from 535 were selected. The screening factors for selecting questionnaires for gathering meaningful data were gleaned from the following questions: (1) Does the respondent currently supervise employees? and (2) Does he have a problem employee?" Clay-Yates, p. 23.

[4] Clay-Yates, p. 6.

[5] Clay-Yates, p. 67.

[6] John Naisbett, "The Bottom-Up Society: America Between Eras," *Public Opinion*, April-May 1981, p. 19.

[7] "In the nineteen seventies, all national surveys showed an increase in preoccupation with self. By the late seventies, my firm's studies showed more than seven out of ten Americans [72%] spent a great deal of time thinking about themselves and their inner lives--this in a nation once notorious for its impatience with inwardness. The rage for self-fulfillment, our surveys indicated, had now spread to virtually the entire U.S. population." Daniel Yankelovich, *New Rules: Searching for Self-Fulfillment in a World Turned Upside Down* (New York: Random House, 1981), p. 5.

[8] *The Challenge of Crime in a Free Society*, A Report by the U.S. President's Commission on Law Enforcement and Administration of Justice, U.S. Government Printing Office,

Washington, D.C., p. 109. The Commission recommends: "The ultimate aim of all police departments should be that all personnel with general enforcement powers have baccalaureate degrees."

[9] Michael T. Farmer, ed., *Survey of Police Operational and Administrative Practices--1977* (Washington, D.C.: Police Executive Research Forum, 1978), p. 63.

[10] Daniel J. Levinson, *The Seasons of a Man's Life* (New York: Alfred A. Knopf, 1978).

[11] Yankelovich, p. 238.

[12] Frederick Herzberg says there are two elements which create employee motivation—the job itself and the hygiene factors. He describes hygiene factors as those things and circumstances incidental to work itself, such as salary, fringe benefits, working conditions supervision, policies, procedures, rules, and regulations. These can be viewed either as positive or negative and can cause dissatisfaction or satisfaction but cannot be viewed as motivators because true motivation, according to Herzberg, comes from the job itself, its scope, its values, and the sense of accomplishment it provides.

[13] U.S. President's Commission, 1967, p. 91; Farmer, p. 13.

[14] George S. Odiorne, *The Change Resisters* (Englewood Cliffs, N.J.: Prentice-Hall, Inc., 1981), p. 16.

[15] Daniel J. Bell, "The Police-Personnel Upgrading for Professionalism," *The Police Chief*, Vol. XLV, No. 1, January 1978, p. 32.

[16] Clay-Yates, p. 65.

Evaluation: A Tool for Management

By Richard C. Sonnichsen
and
Gustave A. Schick

How many times have you made a major policy decision wishing you had more or better information? Have you often wanted more time to study an issue before deciding on a course of action? Have you ever, in exasperation, believed your decisionmaking process could best be described as "muddling through"?[1] Are you sometimes skeptical of claims made by your managers citing the success of programs under their direction? This article will describe a technique to increase the amount and quality of information you need to better manage your resources, improve your decisionmaking process, and reduce the level of uncertainty in the management process.

Law enforcement functions in a complex environment. Policy decision by managers are often subject to intense review and scrutiny, not only by those immediately affected within the organization but also by the public and media. Difficult decisions made on complex issues within short time frames often preclude indepth research. Policy making is never a clear cut process, seldom presents clear choices, and usually results in compromises among many options. Many times we "muddle through" the decisionmaking process with insufficient information. Information may be available to assist the decisionmaker but is not used because it is unavailable at the time or in an unusable form.

The effectiveness and productivity of important programs may go undetermined because of a lack of suitable measurement criteria. Programs implemented for a legitimate cause may be left unattended and become stagnant and ineffective or drift away from their original intent. Programs with merit sometimes never become effective because of faulty design or improper implementation. "Ideas in good currency" fail to even reach program status because they lie buried under layers of bureaucracy, unable to surface due to the lack of a suitable management mechanism for review.

Evaluation is the management technique that can help alleviate these problems and aid the decisionmaker. The thesis of this article is that the technique of program evaluation can assist managers and administrators in making better informed decisions and reduce uncertainty about programs by furnishing relevant, useful information in a timely fashion.

Program evaluation has been defined as the "application of systematic research methods to the assessment of program design, implementation and effectiveness."[2] Although this definition accurately describes the business of program evaluation, our view of evaluation is broader and places an evaluation staff in the role of an internal management consulting firm. In addition to evaluation activities, the skills and experience of an evaluation staff can be used in a variety of problem-solving situations and is a valuable resource for managers.[3]

The FBI Experience

Formal, structured evaluation in the FBI began in 1972 with the formation of the Office of Planning and Evaluation (OPE), with six Special Agents reporting to an Assistant Director. The purpose of the office at that time was to serve in an advisory capacity to the Director of the FBI, coordinate Bureauwide planning, promote research and development, evaluate plans and policy, and conduct surveys and studies.[4] Since that time, the size of the staff has fluctuated between 6 and 14, with evaluators selected from the ranks of Special Agent investigators who are potential candidates for executive positions in the Bureau.

In our opinion, the advantages of an in-house evaluation staff outweigh the use of outside consultants for the FBI. Using experienced Special Agents as evaluators brings instant credibility when conducting interviews with other Agents. The Agent evaluator also has knowledge of the structure and administration of the FBI, and due to his varied experience, has a working knowledge of most of the investigative programs to be evaluated.

Evaluators in the FBI are used primarily in three different ways: (1) in a classic evaluation sense: reviewing major investigative programs on a 5-year cycle; (2) as policy analysts, studying topics selected by top management with a short response time; and (3) as management consultants, reviewing specific management problems to determine the most effective and efficient means to manage. The majority of projects chosen for evaluation or study originate from an annual survey of field executives; however, some studies are self-initiated by the staff where a problem has surfaced during other evaluation activities.

Although the FBI evaluation staff is organizationally located in the Inspection Division reporting to the Director, evaluation is distinct from the inspection function and should not be confused with it. While the usual purpose of an inspection is to check compliance and determine responsibility where deficiencies are encountered, evaluation has as its purpose program improvement. Successful evaluations are conducted in a spirit of cooperation with the program manager contributing input throughout the evaluation. Numerous studies have shown,[5] and our experience validates, that use of evaluation findings by affected decisionmakers is significantly dependent on cooperation during the evaluation process and the extent of involvement of the individual program manager.

Much of the available literature on evaluation refers to "evaluation research." The word "research," used in conjunction with evaluation, evokes a strong, negative reaction in the minds of many executives who fear they will be overwhelmed and intimidated by the material presented. Use of this terminology creates unnecessary impediments to the use of evaluation findings. Usefulness should be the major criterion for measuring evaluation findings. Meeting the informational needs of the decisionmaker is of paramount importance and should be the goal of the evaluator. The policy maker's questions should drive the evaluation process. It is the responsibility of the evaluator to produce information that is timely, relevant, and in a form easily understood by the user. Complex statistical analysis can be counterproductive and is seldom necessary.[6] A noted evaluation author, Michael Quinn Patton, has said, "I would rather have 'soft data' on important questions than 'hard data' on unimportant questions."[7]

Evaluation can be used to effect organizational change. Our experience has been that program change usually begins when an evaluation starts and is not dependent on the completion or issuance of a report. The analysis of programs and objectives can redefine and sharpen policy procedures, thereby creating a more effective and efficient organization. Monitoring program output makes information available on resource usage that can affect future manpower distribution patterns. Quantitative data from information systems can be illuminated with qualitative data gathered by experienced evaluators through indepth interviews of program managers and participants.

Establishing an Evaluation Staff

Before committing to the concept of evaluation as a management tool, you, as a law enforcement executive, should conduct a mini-evaluation of your own. You need to reflect on your style of management and leadership and the environment of your department to determine if this technique might be of assistance. Contemplating your own situation is critical before establishing an evaluation staff. To assist in making this decision, we have developed a nine-point diagnostic test to determine if an evaluation group could be of assistance.

1) Am I comfortable with the quality and quantity of information I have available to make major decisions?
2) Am I sufficiently knowledgeable of all major aspects of my department to make informed decisions?
3) Do I know if my policies and programs are being practiced or given lip service?
4) Are my programs efficient and effective and do I have a system for feedback on program performance?

5) Am I comfortable with the productivity levels of units under my command?

6) Do I have sufficient information available to me to judge comprehensively the performance of my subordinates?

7) Do I have a selection method for identifying potential top executives?

8) Is any part of my department responsible for organizational change or program improvements?

9) Is my managerial style such that I would solicit and use information from an evaluation group if I had one?

Asking yourself these questions should assist in defining the current state of organizational development in your department and force you to examine not only the organizational climate but your own management style. The questions are designed to establish a mental, schematic diagram of the information availability, flow, and usage in your organization.

An evaluation staff will divert some resources from other areas. The critical question then is cost effectiveness. Although difficult to measure, criteria can be established to determine the effectiveness of evaluation activities.

A few examples from our experience may help demonstrate the value of evaluation. A major philosophical shift in the FBI's approach to investigative activities occurred in the mid-1970's and was made possible by a staff of evaluators responding to a mandate from newly appointed FBI Director Clarence M. Kelley to examine the FBI's management structure and traditional approach to investigations. This multi-year project in OPE resulted in a resource management and utilization concept. It was aided by an information system which redirected limited Agent resources to the most significant criminal investigations.

An evaluation of the FBI's foreign language program determined its administration was divided among four divisions at FBI Headquarters. Recommendations to consolidate all functions under one division have increased the effectiveness and efficiency of the program. Evaluation of the methodology used to determine the training needs of our veteran investigators has improved that procedure. An evaluation of the management of FBI resident agencies (small offices outside of a headquarters city) recommended three options for managing these offices to maximize productivity and insure proper workload distribution. Recent evaluations of our property crimes, fugitive, and general government crimes investigative programs resulted in recommendations to increase the efficient use of available manpower. Automation of indices, Special Agent transfer policy, and procedures for conducting background investigations are examples of administrative evaluations we conduct.

The Evaluation Unit is structured to examine quickly policy issues of concern to top management, and a 30-day turnaround time on these studies is not uncommon. The evaluation staff was recently requested to analyze the staffing and organizational structure of one of the FBI's regional computer centers. Neither complex in design nor scientifically rigorous, these short studies nevertheless aid the decisionmaker by furnishing him timely, relevant data.

The value of the evaluation process does not rely solely on the conduct of the study and the issuance of a report. It has been our experience that the mere presence of the evaluators causes managers to re-evaluate their programs, and many times, issue their own recommendations for program improvement long before the completion of the evaluation.

Organizing for Evaluation

Be clear on purpose — Before the first line is drawn on an organization chart and before the first personnel file is reviewed for candidates, the purpose of the staff you are about to form should be very clear in your mind. Evaluation staffs can be used effectively in a variety of ways—as personal emissaries of the chief, as independent auditors, as an internal consulting staff to aid in the development of programs, or in any of an endless number of variations on these themes. Additionally, some evaluation staffs complete their evaluation activities with a written and/or oral report of their findings and make no recommendations for improvement; others make recommendations based on their findings, while still others not only make recommendations but get actively involved in implementation. The correct mode is the one which fits best with your personal managerial style and philosophy. What is important is that the manner in which the evaluation staff will be used and the purpose to which it will be put are clear at the outset and made clear to the staff. While there may be legitimate political and bureaucratic reasons to use an evaluation staff to legitimize decisions which have already been made, such use will quickly become apparent to the staff and others and is not a sound way to attract and keep talented people.

Locate staff correctly — Once you have conceptualized the purpose of the evaluation staff, you must locate it correctly within the organizational structure. We have found that the fewer layers of bureaucracy between the evaluation unit and the chief executive officer, the better. The fewer information filters between the evaluators and the executive, the less distortion you will hear. We have also found that obtaining information is generally facilitated when the evaluation staff is perceived as operating with a direct mandate from the top. If you should choose to locate the evaluation unit further down in the organizational ladder, you should take steps to communicate personally and directly with the staff periodically in order to be aware of what they are doing and let them know of your concerns and support. An evaluation unit can be your eyes and ears, stay in close touch with them.

Staff well — The success or failure of your evaluation staff will depend to a large extent on the caliber of the people you choose. A good evaluator should have a broad range of experience and skills. He should be innovative and creative, critical and analytical, with a strong bias against "we've always done it that way" reasoning. He must be able to express himself well orally and in writing. Ideally, he should have an educational and/or professional background in management with a facility for using statistical and other quantitative techniques. Finally, he should be a sworn officer with sufficient time on the street to give him a thorough understanding of police work and credibility with fellow officers with whom he will have to interact. The evaluation staff in the FBI is comprised exclusively of Special Agents. While we occasionally sacrifice some technical expertise, we believe this is more than offset by the Agents' understanding of the nature of our work and the credibility these Agents have in the organization.

How many individuals are appropriate to staff your evaluation unit depends, of course, on the size of your department and the resources you have available. We believe a critical mass for an effective evaluation unit is probably three individuals; one or two people will not have the dynamic interaction which generates creative thought processes and innovative solutions to problems.

Choose appropriate subjects — Take care in choosing issues for your evaluation unit to review, particularly at the outset while the staff is still getting its legs. The primary criterion is that issues should be something you care about. Nothing will destroy the morale of an evaluation unit faster, and cost it more credibility, than being assigned meaningless tasks or assignments which everyone concerned knows have no solution. Avoid the temptation to duck a difficult issue by saying "we have that under study." You may wish eventually to have all functional areas of the department evaluated on a cyclical basis; however, at the outset, pick areas that are of primary concern and where you will feel comfortable implementing changes.

Tasking

Now that you have defined the evaluation unit's purpose, located it within the organization, staffed it, and chosen initial subjects for evaluation, you must inform the staff of what you expect and how you expect it to be accomplished.

Focus on utility — While the investigation of esoteric subjects and the pursuit of knowledge for knowledge's sake is attractive in an academic atmosphere, the focus of evaluation efforts should be on the usefulness of the information developed. You will find one of the primary complaints of the evaluator is "nobody *uses* our product." Minimize this frustration and capitalize on your valuable evaluation resources by encouraging your staff to bear in mind constantly the importance of developing information that is useful to you as a decision-maker, not elegant research models and sophisticated analytic techniques.

Insist that your evaluation staff be objective, rigorous, and complete in their review of any set of activities, but do not demand that they always be "scientifically rigorous." While questions of causality and "replicability" are important to scientists, you are primarily interested in gaining objective information to improve your decisionmaking in an imperfect world. An exception to this would be in a situation where the basis for your decision may be challenged in court and you may be required to demonstrate the validity of the data. The development of hiring standards is an example of an area where you may wish to take pains to ensure the research is done in a scientifically supportable fashion.

Insist on time limits and clarity — Information is a perishable commodity, and the most accurate data analyzed in the most elegant fashion is useless if it arrives after a decision has already been made. We have found that without a sense of urgency from top management, evaluation projects can take an ever-increasing amount of time as new issues develop demanding further and further study. Set deadlines and insist they be met.

By the same token, evaluation results that lack clarity are not usable to you as a decisionmaker, and in the worst case, can add to the confusion they are meant to reduce. Whether you choose oral briefings, written reports, or what we have found to be most effective, a combination of the two, demand that evaluation results be presented to you in a clear, jargon-free, and concise fashion.

Make recommendations — Some evaluators take the position that their responsibility stops with the presentation of findings. We have found that taking the extra step and making recommendations for action is worthwhile. The evaluator is usually more familiar with the details of a particular issue and is in a better position to craft a recommendation than the executive. Once approved by the executive, the recommendations take on the character of directives.

Keep in mind also that over the period of the evaluation, much information comes to the attention of the evaluator that never reaches the final report and opinions are formed that cannot always be documented in a rigorous way. Although many evaluators are reluctant to comment outside the scope of the report, don't hesitate to solicit their opinions for they may be of value to you.[8] An advocacy role supporting the recommendations in an evaluation does not compromise the evaluator, if the evaluation was conducted in an objective and unbiased manner.[9]

Follow up — Like other directives, some approved recommendations are implemented and some seem to fall through a crack. In the FBI, we contact the entity to whom the recommendations are directed 6 months following approval. We do sufficient review at that time to assure ourselves that the recommendation either has been implemented or over-riding circumstances have made it either impossible or counter-productive. Our studies are not closed until all approved recommendations have been brought to closure.

Evaluation Process

Certain features are common to most, if not all, evaluations, and you should have an idea what to expect from the process.[10]

Literature Review

The evaluation staff will familiarize itself with the subject matter under review and determine what research has already been done in the area. Typically, the review of available literature will include manuals, policy files, internal memoranda, a review of data from internal management information systems, and if applicable, academic research done in the area. The literature review will help define the scope and objectives of the evaluation and should assist the staff greatly in choosing an evaluation strategy.

Evaluation Plan

Following the literature review, the evaluator in charge of the study should develop an evaluation plan. We have found this to be a critical document, because it forces the evaluator to focus his thinking and reduce to paper exactly what he intends to accomplish and how he intends to accomplish it. The plan should contain, at a minimum, the purpose of the study, the scope, specific objectives that will be accomplished, a detailed statement of the methods by which various questions will be addressed, and a proposed time table with specific due dates for various phases of the project. This plan should be reviewed by the official requesting the study to ensure that his concerns are being addressed adequately.

Data Gathering

Once the study plan has been approved, the next phase is generally data gathering. In the FBI, this often includes field visits to a representative number of our 59 field divisions. Data gathering can take many forms, such as reviews of incident reports and case files, observation, interview, and questionnaires. If your staff is skilled, you should not have to be overly concerned with this phase of the project. You should, however, caution your staff that all data gathering, particularly interviews, should be conducted in an unbiased manner so as to convey the impression that the evaluation team has no ax to grind nor has made up its mind as to the outcome before the evaluation is complete.

Analysis and Report Writing

At the conclusion of the data gathering phase, you can expect the evaluation staff to consume about as much time as it took them to gather the data to analyze and report their findings. You should require a written report, supplemented if you wish by an oral briefing. If you have given your evaluation staff the mandate to make recommendations, we suggest the recommendations be set forth in a memorandum separate from the evaluation report. This will give you the flexibility to approve or not approve various recommendations without affecting the findings of the evaluation which are reflected in the report.

Conflict

One byproduct of many evaluations which you should expect is conflict. New ways of doing things, new ways of looking at information, and new ways of defining success can threaten people. A natural resistance to change may manifest itself in the rejection of the evaluation's findings by those whose area of responsibility has been evaluated. You will occasionally hear a host of counter arguments as to why proposed changes are not feasible. Kept within professional bounds, such conflict is healthy for it forces managers to articulate the reasons things are done the way they are and it can point out fallacies in the evaluation staff's rea-

soning and conclusions. Don't be afraid of conflict, manage it.

How to Tell If It's Working

The efficacy of an evaluation staff is, to a large degree, in the eye of the beholder. If you as chief executive and user of the product think the staff is producing the desired results, they probably are. Although this is a subjective criterion for success, it can be supplemented with quantifiable data. Recommendations approved and implemented and program improvements are two additional criteria that can be used in determining the success of an evaluation staff.

It can sometimes be difficult to demonstrate a cause-and-effect relationship between the work done by an evaluation staff and changes in operations. Very often, the change process begins as soon as the evaluators appear on the scene and begin asking questions. By the time the study is completed and the report written, a great many changes may have taken place, none of which will be attributed to the evaluators. It simply does not seem to be human nature for a manager to run into his chief's office and announce, "My narcotics operation was floundering, but those guys doing that evaluation really had some good ideas and things are a lot better now!" More likely you'll hear, "Well we had some problems but we knew all about them and were going ahead with our own solutions when that evaluation began." Does it matter who's right? Probably not. The important thing is that problems were uncovered and corrected. Who gets the public credit is really immaterial, frustrating to the evaluators, but immaterial.

What is material is that the product being produced, the findings and recommendations, is useful to your department. Utility is the primary criterion you should apply in evaluating the evaluation process. Look for work that is on point, recommendations that are feasible, and an attitude that fosters cooperative action.

Conclusion

The technique of evaluation can be a powerful tool for aiding managers in the decisionmaking process and determining organizational performance. In creating an evaluation staff, if you have done your work well and have brought together the right people, tasked them clearly and correctly, held them to high standards, and supported them, you will have given your department an added dimension for development, that of self-examination and critical review.

About the Authors

Richard C. Sonnichsen is the Deputy Assistant Director, Inspection Division, assigned to FBI Headquarters, Washington, D.C. He heads the Office of Program Evaluations and Audits which conducts evaluations and financial audits in the FBI. He has a B.S. degree from the University of Idaho and is a doctoral candidate in public administration at the University of Southern California. His areas of interest are internal evaluation and evaluation utilization.

Gus Schick is the Assistant Inspector General in charge of the Office of Labor Racketeering, U.S. Department of Labor. Formerly a special Agent of the FBI, Mr. Schick was the Chief of the Program Evaluations Unit in the FBI's Inspection Division. Mr. Schick holds a B.S. degree in mathematics from Duke University and a M.B.A. in Operations Analysis from the American University.

Footnotes

[1] Charles E. Lindblom, "The Science of 'Muddling Through,'" *Classics of Public Administration*, eds. Jay M. Shafritz and Albert C. Hyde (Oak Park, IL: Moore Publishing Co., Inc., 1978), pp. 202-213. Lindblom claims administrators are incapable of analyzing the vast amount of information relevant to a given situation.

[2] Elinor Chelimsky, ed., *Program Evaluation: Patterns and Directions* (Washington, DC: ASPA PAR Classics VI, 1985).

[3] For an examination of the role of the internal consultant, as well as the external consulting process, see Gordon Lippitt and Ronald Lippitt, *The Consulting Process in Action* (San Diego, CA: University Associates, Inc., 1978).

[4] From policy files maintained by the FBI's Office of Program Evaluations and Audits.

[5] Michael Quinn Patton, *Utilization-Focused Evaluations* (Beverly Hills, CA: Sage Publications, 1978) (Patton calls this the "personal factor"); Ray C. Oman and Stephan R. Chitwood, "Management Evaluation Studies, Factors Affecting the Acceptance of Recommendations," *Evaluation Review*, Vol. 8, No. 3, June 1984, pp. 283-305; Judith A. Dawson and Joseph J. D'Amico, "Involving Program Staff in Evaluation Studies, A Strategy for Increasing Information Use and Enriching the Data Base," *Evaluation Review*, Vol. 9, No. 2, April 1985, pp. 173-188; Karolynn Siegel and Peter Tuckel, "The Utilization of Evaluation Research," *Evaluation Review*, Vol. 9, No. 3, June 1985, pp. 307-328.

[6] Martin Kotler, "Conducting Short-term Policy Evaluation Studies in the Real World," a paper presented at the Evaluation Research Society Conference in San Francisco, CA, October 1984.

[7] Michael Quinn Patton at an evaluation workshop conducted at the FBI Academy, Quantico, VA, 4/17-18/85.

[8] From an address by Hale Champion, Executive Dean, John F. Kennedy School of Government, Harvard University, to a joint meeting of The Evaluation Research Society and The Evaluation Network, October 11, 1984, San Francisco, CA.

[9] We frequently become involved in the policy-making process, upon completion of an evaluation, attending meetings, writing memoranda, preparing briefings, and advising line managers all in support of the findings and recommendations.

[10] Many of these features are more fully described in *Evaluation Basics, A Practitioner's Manual*, Jacqueline Kosecoff and Arlene Fink (Beverly Hills, CA: Sage Publications, 1982).

CHAPTER IV
COUNSELING

INTRODUCTION TO CHAPTER IV:
Counseling

Giving advice to and getting advice from police personnel keeps departments in touch with their greatest resource: People. This chapter focuses on the much-needed dialogue between department and personnel and offers innovative models of communication that can improve any department.

Article 13, by James W. Skidmore, details a workable and efficient method to address the communications problems within all organizations, especially law enforcement agencies. The employee council, which the author describes, consists of employees from all the ranks in the department. Such a cross-section ensures communication throughout the department. The author provides a model that would serve to improve communication within any department.

In Article 14, F. L. Capps describes how law enforcement officers experience traumatic incidents in their lives and thus, need a release valve. He argues that incidents such as auto accidents, shootings, and personal tragedies can be countered by a good peer counseling program. Using the Los Angeles Police Department's program as a model, Capps outlines how the program works, its goals, its training component, and how management relates to it.

Article 15, by Roger L. Depue, Ph.D., accurately describes the law enforcement job as demanding and describes law enforcement officers as needing some balance in their lives. Depue maintains that the police personnel must maintain a balance between three perspectives: individual, family, and occupation. And indeed, keeping this balance is difficult, with the family often losing out to the occupational component.

In Article 16, authors Thomas Ammann and Paul Meyer argue that perhaps the most neglected aspect of career development is retirement—the end of one's career. They offer the Cincinnati Police Department's preretirement program as a viable model for other departments. Their program puts officers

and their families in touch with experts in health, insurance, and with a host of areas important to the retirees and their families. Such programs also extend the very clear message to employees: that the department cares about its personnel from their first day on the job to their last.

In Article 17, Thomas J. Deakin, J.D., presents his thesis in the very first line: "Police Service in America was, and is today, exactly that—a service." He gives us a glimpse back at where we've been, examines where we are now, and looks at where we are going with personnel in the law enforcement profession.

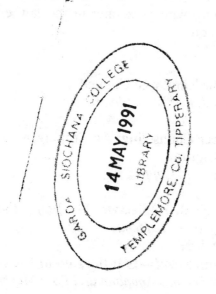

The Employee Council

By James W. Skidmore

One of the greatest difficulties in administering a police department is ensuring that there is a two-way flow of necessary information within the organizational structure. Police departments, and police officers in general, seem to be affected by rumors or false information much more than other organizations. Therefore, it is critical that correct information be disseminated *and* understood. In many departments, this problem is magnified by the administration, the working unit, or both. Thus, finding a better way to communicate within the organization will make attaining departmental objectives and goals more likely.

In talking with various officers within the department, it became apparent that there also was a lack of communication among the various units. Patrol officers complained that detectives took information given the officers and were seldom informed as to the value of that information or the status of the case. If the information was used to clear up various offenses, the investigators failed to give the patrol officers what they regarded as "just dues." In addition, there was a lack of communication between patrol shifts, which was fostered by the fact that there was no shift rotation and officers were unaware of the other shift's problems or responsibilities.

Unfortunately, this lack of intimate communication is prevalent in a majority of police departments, if we look at the issue honestly. And, the problems cited previously exist within other units of a police department—records, communications, evidence, detective, patrol, and management.

The West Bend Police Department, in order to ensure a free flow of information within its organization, carefully reviewed its internal information system, seeking ways to increase understanding, cooperation, and feedback. We considered concepts not necessarily tied to law enforcement, but which had a successful impact on the organization. As a result, a concept called the "employee council" was adopted and implemented within our department.

The employee council consist of employees representing each division within the police department. Members rotate quarterly among those interested in serving on the council, and meetings are held monthly.

The purpose of the employee council is to promote intradepartmental cooperation and to open the lines for communication throughout the department. Awareness of, and appreciation for, each other's concerns, problems, and expectations are vital in establishing and maintaining positive relationships essential in achieving goals and objectives.

The council consists of eight members, including four patrol officers, one from each shift and relief shift, one Support Services technician, one investigator, and two staff members. The members are selected from those officers and employees willing to be a part of this council. Each of the three shifts of the Patrol Division and the relief shift elects its own representative, as do the Support Services and Investigative Units. The two staff members are appointed by the chief from first-line supervisors and commanders and provide input from the supervisory and administrative perspective. Because they attend monthly staff meetings, these staff members know why decisions were made, and many times, this information is valuable at the employee council meetings to defuse potential problems and rumors.

Once employees are selected for the council, an election is held to select a presiding chairperson for that quarter and a secretary. The only restriction placed on the council by the chief was that no staff member could be elected as chairperson or secretary. Council members are encouraged to make every effort possible to attend scheduled meetings;

however, if a member is unable to do so, he/she can select an alternate from his/her respective division or unit.

Minutes taken at all meetings are typed, copied, and distributed in order that all department employees are kept informed of council activities and discussions. Copies are sent to the chief of police, command staff, patrol officers, roll call board, records and communications roll call board, and the Investigative Unit's office.

After each employee council meeting, the chairperson meets with the chief of police to provide an overview of council concerns and topics of discussion. Either the chief and/or the appropriate division commander provides written response to the issues raised in writing, usually within 30 days.

Every employee of the department is encouraged to make suggestions that will improve performance, efficiency, effectiveness, and safety. Their input is valuable in terms of providing different perspectives to problems that may not be readily identifiable at the management level. The mere criticism of a particular method, procedure, or piece of equipment is not sufficient to initiate change in a rational and responsible manner. All facts and circumstances as they affect the overall organization must be taken into consideration to ensure that the suggestion achieves the objective of actually causing improvement. Therefore, certain procedures were initiated so that each suggestion would be evaluated objectively.

All suggestions have to be submitted in the form of completed staff work, so that nothing remains to be done except for approval or disapproval by the final authority. To satisfy the criteria of completed staff work, a suggestion must include the following:

1) Introduction: A statement of the circumstances prompting the suggestion.
2) Problem Statement: An accurate definition of what the problem is and the effect it has on the department. This should be a factual statement substantiated by adequate research and not assumption.
3) Alternative Solutions: Statement of the available solutions that will remedy the problem and the identification of the best solution that is the most cost effective and practical. This also includes a statement of how the suggestion will affect the department as a whole, which should be substantiated by adequate research.
4) Cost Analysis: A breakdown of any cost involved for equipment or personnel.
5) Method of Implementation: A statement of what the means of implementing this suggestion would be, i.e., new procedure, purchasing request, directive, etc.
6) Summary: A statement of all the facts that support the recommendation.

Only those suggestions submitted in the prescribed format will be given further consideration, since planning and research personnel are not available to do the necessary followup work. If the suggestion is not acceptable in total, but still has some merit, that part of the suggestion will be responded to in writing.

The West Bend Police Department has been using this concept for the past several years and has found it to be highly effective in improving communications, both among the various units within the department and between shifts and the working unit and management. However, for this program to be successful, there must be a firm commitment from the administration, the supervisors, and the employees themselves.

The commitment of the administration is such that a police department facility is used for the meetings. Those officers off duty when the meeting is scheduled are paid overtime to attend the meeting; those on duty are excused from their station to attend. Clerical personnel are available to type minutes and other paperwork necessary to submit a suggestion properly. Also, all resources of the department are available for research and development of the possible suggestions.

Commitment of the employees is another essential element. Employees must be willing to serve as members of the council working to improve the efficiency and effectiveness of the department. They must be willing to offer suggestions and to evaluate those submitted to the council for consideration. Rejecting suggestions and informing other employees of the rejections is another responsibility they must be willing to assume. If employees perceive this council as a valuable concept, they will use it. If suggestions for improvement are not generated, it is because the commitment from the employees is not there.

Many of the suggestions that have come from the employee council have dealt with minor issues that cause morale problems, simply because the administration was not given proper feedback by either the staff or first-line supervisors. Changes have been made in certain procedures or orders that have alleviated the concerns of employees. The members of the council have also rejected suggestions because they were not in the best interests of the entire department. Through this concept of the employee council, the employees have a legitimate recourse to initiate change within the department, instead of the informal system that usually brings about change but with a negative manner and most times outside the guidelines of the department.

Summary

Everyone benefits from a more efficient and effective police department. However, for the employee council to be successful, it takes a total commitment on the part of the administration and the employees. The employee council opens lines of communication within a department and is another vehicle to improve operations and to meet departmental goals and objectives. The council allows employees to have the opportunity to provide input into the decisionmaking process and institute change when appropriate.

About the Author

James W. Skidmore is Chief of Police of the West Bend, Wisconsin, Police Department. He has held that position for the past ten years. Formerly he was on the Mt. Lebanon, Pennsylvania, Police Force for nineteen years. Chief Skidmore holds a B.A. degree in Administration of Justice from the University of Pittsburgh, and an A.S. degree from Allegheney County Community College in Police Science and Administration. He is a graduate of the FBI Academy. He attended Southern Police Institute and other police related advanced schools. Currently he is on the faculty of Waukesha County Technical College in Waukesha, Wisconsin, and Moraine Park Technical College in Fond du Lac, Wisconsin.

Peer Counseling: An Employee Assistance Program

By F.L. Capps

A primary challenge to law enforcement in the United States today is employee occupational stress overload. In a recent survey of U.S. law enforcement agencies, conducted by the FBI's Training Division, the top 10 training priorities were identified. First among them was "personal stress."[1]

Stress affects us all—in the public sector, in private life, in the ranks of law enforcement, and at the top. In a 1982 interview, Los Angeles Police Chief Daryl Gates revealed that like his officers, he too feels stress. Gates called the nearly 4 years he has served as chief "the most frustrating, discouraging period in my life."[2]

Stress is a major problem affecting law enforcement administrators today. Its overt effects can be seen in the high percentage of officers who have experienced stress-related illnesses and in its other critical socio-cultural manifestations, such as increased alcohol use and a high rate of divorce.[3]

There is a large volume of research material available today on the occupational stresses police officers face. Roger Depue, Chief of the Behavioral Science Unit at the FBI Academy, points to the following major problem areas which impact on occupational stress: ambiguity in the role of the police officer in today's complex society; problems adapting to the work environment when it involves a subculture, ethnic group, or lifestyle different from his own; conflict in separating his onduty activities from his personal life and maintaining a balance in allocating time to both; and the situational crisis brought on by the trauma associated with a death, serious injury, or a shooting incident. In addition, Depue points to the frustration of numerous "organizational factors," including poor equipment, lack of administrative support, and departmental disciplinary action.[4]

A 1975 study of police officers in Virginia found that the typical officer is exposed to an injured adult three times each month, a severe assault victim every 45 days, and a dead person every 3 months.[5]

A National Institute of Occupational Safety and Health study reported that 37 percent of the police studied had serious marital problems, 23 percent had serious alcohol problems, and 10 percent had significant drug problems. The study went on to note that policemen have a significantly higher rate of early death than the general population and rank third among all occupations in suicide.[6]

EMPLOYEE ASSISTANCE PROGRAMS

Corporate Programs

Programs that provide various types of assistance to employees are not new to either the public or private sectors of the United States. About 1 out of 5 of the Fortune 500 companies now have some sort of stress management program. Many of these programs are restricted to top executives even though studies have shown that the most stressed workers are in middle management. In addition to facing the pressures of climbing the corporate ladder, these workers are caught in a perilous bind—a lot of responsibility but little control.[7]

Corporate efforts to reduce stress range from the commonplace alcoholism program to onpremise exercise facilities, meditation, and company-sponsored biofeedback classes. At the Equitable Life Insurance Company in Manhattan, employees with frequent stress-related health complaints participated in an inhouse biofeedback program and reduced their average number of visits to the company medical office from 24 to fewer than 6 annually. Equitable saved $5.52 in medical costs for every $1 invested.[8]

At New York Telephone, a program involving periodic health exams for all employees and meditation lessons for those with stress-related symptoms has helped cut the corporate hypertension rate from 18 percent—about average for U.S. firms—to half that amount. New York Telephone estimates that it is saving $130,000 a year from reduced absenteeism alone.[9]

FBI Employee Assistance Programs

In the FBI's New York Office, a pilot program was established in 1977 for alcoholism and related problems. The program offered confidential assistance to employees who had alcohol problems that may be causing declines in job performance. The program used voluntary assistance from recovering alcoholics among New York Office employees and achieved great success in eliciting self-referral by employees suffering alcoholism problems. In 1981, about 45 employees sought assistance from the New York Office program. Of this number, 27 were self-referrals, and 18 were management-initiated referrals. By the end of the year, 28 had been restored to full performance; only 3 had failed to respond favorably.[10] Based upon the success of the New York pilot program, the program was implemented Bureauwide.

In a continuing effort to recognize and respond to employee needs, the FBI in early 1982 established a contractual agreement with two mental health professionals, Dr. David A. Soskis, M.D. and Dr. Carole W. Soskis, M.S.W., J.D., who provide psychiatric assistance to FBI employees who voluntarily seek help and psychological service consultation in administrative and operational matters. These two professionals handle a wide range of individual employee psychological problems either personally or by a system of referrals to psychologists who practice in the area where the employee resides. They also identify stressors that negatively affect job performance and design programs to impact on stress management. Employees may seek psychological assistance or be administratively referred by a supervisor.

A second entity within the FBI which provides psychological services is the Behavioral Science Unit at the FBI Academy. This unit coordinates psychological services in the areas of training and operational support matters. This would include crime analysis, criminal profiling, personality assessment, and occupational stress awareness and management.

Recently, the FBI implemented two new programs designed to impact an area where psychological problems have surfaced. Dr. David Soskis and Dr. Carole Soskis, in coordination with members of the Behavioral Science Unit and Institutional Research Unit, developed psychological guidelines for the supervision of undercover operations. These guidelines were developed to reduce the anger, resentment, and potential for acting out that can accompany prolonged undercover assignments. A second program, which addressed the trauma associated with shooting incidents, was initiated in late 1983. This program provides intervention at the shooting scene, as well as training in prevention and long term followup.

The Los Angeles Police Department Peer Counseling Program

The Los Angeles Police Department (LAPD), like many large city departments, has full-time psychologists on staff, in addition to several of the employee assistance programs discussed above. They have also taken the lead in the initiation of a program of peer assistance or peer counseling. The LAPD is the first department in the country to develop and implement an integrated and fully department-supported peer counseling program using regularly employed officers and civilians on a large scale.[11] It defines peer counseling as "a group of employees who have been to a three day school and have volunteered to give direct, simple support to people who are hurting."[12] Their program has been in existence for 2 years and has a proven track record. It began during the summer of 1981 in response to the major psychological trauma suffered by two LAPD officers as a result of their involvement in shooting incidents. It is important to note, however, that the program goes far beyond providing assistance to officers involved in shootings. Monthly statistics indicate that the majority of counseling time—70 percent—is spent on issues

Month	**January 1984**
Number of Counselors	69
Number of Counseling Hours	469
Number of Clients	191
Counseling Issues:	
a. Personal Relationships (Family stress and divorce)	54
b. Employee alcohol and substance abuses	15
c. Financial	11
d. Bereavement (Death and dying, illness)	20
e. Job Discipline	19
f. Career Advancement Problems	68

Figure 1

involving personal relationships, discipline, and career problems.[13]

Program Goals

There are several goals of a counseling program of this type, including:

1) To help follow employees through the temporary crisis situations that are a common part of our lives;

2) To develop a readily accessible network of employees trained and willing to be of service to their fellow employees who have expressed a need for assistance;

3) To develop an awareness among employees that they are not alone, that people are willing to listen to them, and that others care about them and their problems;

4) To develop among employees an awareness of the self-help alternatives that are available to them;

5) To develop a system of referrals which can provide, in more serious cases, appropriate professional care; and

6) To increase the availability of employees, thereby increasing organizational efficiency, through a program of intervention which can assist in defusing problems before they reach a point of crisis and result in the loss of work-time.

Officer Reaction

Professional inhouse psychological services have been available at LAPD and other larger law enforcement agencies for years. However, many police officers who experience psychological problems do not consider obtaining professional help. This is seen by some to be a reflection of the officer's stereotypical belief that people who seek professional help are seriously ill, out of control, unmanly, or unfit for work.[14] Because police organizations tend generally to be close-knit, officers experiencing personal problems often feel more comfortable discussing these matters with a fellow officer rather than a mental health professional.

Peer Counsel Training

It is often believed that the counseling process requires extensive training and can only be conducted by specialists with advanced degrees. The opposite, however, appears to be true. The effectiveness of the minimally trained paraprofessional versus that of one who has received formal training in the mental health profession is considered in a 1979 paper by Joseph Durlak.[15] Professional mental health training does not appear to be a necessary prerequisite. Paraprofessionals are rated by the studies reviewed at least as effective and often better than professionals.

LAPD's training program for peer counselors is conducted over a 24-hour period by a team consisting of a licensed psychologist, an experienced peer counselor, several guest speakers, and role players. Topics include reflective listening, general assessment skills for distinguishing chronic from short-term problems, problem-solving skills, alcohol and drug abuse problems, the issue of death, dying and relationship termination, suicide risk assessment and management, and when and how to refer.[16] New counselors are given instruction in crisis counseling with maximum emphasis on the practical application of a simple but effective model designed to assist the employee in solving his own problems. During training sessions, new counselors assume alternately the roles of counselor and employee, first with classmates and later with trained, experienced peer counselors who take the role of an employee in need of help. By participating in these work counseling situations, the new counselor is able to see his own strengths and weaknesses, and with coaching, improve his skills.

Problem-solving Model

A three-phase crisis counseling model is presented to the new counselors. In the first and most important phase, the hurting employee is given as much time as is necessary to express his feelings. The counselor is taught to provide a non-judgmental, emotionally supportive atmosphere using simple, positive listening skills to facilitate the employee's full discussion of the problem. In the second phase of this model, the counselor assesses the problem presented by the employee and verbally summarizes the points he has heard. This ensures that the counselor has fully heard the employee and that they are in agreement on all of the issues. In the last phase, options are discussed. In most cases, these options are selected by the employee who also makes his own decision concerning which option seems to be best.

Role of Management

The role of supervisors and administrators in this program is extremely important. They should be aware of how the program operates and must believe it to be beneficial to both their subordinates and the organization. Employees involved in counseling will need support and sometimes guidance from supervisory personnel, making it imperative that management at all levels be familiar and supportive of the program. It is also crucial that managers recognize that this program belongs to employees. Its success at LAPD is, in part, due to the fact that it was organized at the "grass roots level" by employees for employees and is not a

management tool used to control employees or a conduit for information to be passed to management. In an interview, Chief Gates addressed this issue, saying, "I must tell you I'm kind of letting this thing grow on its own. I haven't reached down and tried to direct it because I think I could very quickly ruin the whole program just by saying, 'Okay, now I'm going to take control over it and we're going to do it my way.' I may not have the intention, but it might appear that way. I've let it develop on its own."[17]

Confidentiality Issue

Peer counselors have no legally protected privilege of patient confidentiality as do most members of the mental health profession. Even without this legally recognized privilege, a high degree of confidentiality in a program of this type is necessary for its success. The regulations that govern the operation of the LAPD's Peer Counseling Program state that counselors have a responsibility to insure the confidentiality of their communications with employees, with the exception of situations involving criminal acts or violations of department regulations. This limited confidentiality is considered central to the effectiveness of the program.[18]

Conclusion

The time between when an employee begins to experience the minor problems caused by the daily stresses of life and those problems developing to the point where the employee must seek help from a mental health professional is vast. During this period, the employee experiences pain and may make many bad decisions. It is also during this period that a network of peer counselors, acting as paraprofessionals, can step in to give early aid in assisting the employee in resolving his problem, or in severe cases, refer the employee to appropriate professional assistance.

Many acts committed by employees that require a disciplinary response from management are "cries for help." These acts may include shoplifting, drug abuse, alcoholism, or other equally undesirable activities. While peer counselors would be expected to refer these more complicated problems to full-time professionals, they are in a position to detect them early. Early detection and referral has the obvious benefit of preventing major problems later on.

Alcoholism programs involving peer counseling focus on one major issue—alcoholism. With a peer counseling program of the type the LAPD instituted, the focus is expanded to include a wider range of employee problems. These programs can increase productivity, reduce absenteeism, reduce grievances and the need of the disciplinary action, and improve employee morale. Improved employee morale is considered by many to be the most important benefit derived from such programs. A peer counseling program gives concrete evidence to employees that management does care.

Informal peer counseling is common among employees in law enforcement as well as other professions. Employees discuss their problems with their peers, from the most insignificant daily issues to the major life traumas. A study of officers involved in shootings indicates that "a significant phenomenon is that every police officer interviewed was, within 48 hours, back at the station to speak with his fellow officers."[19] Without proper training, however, the results of these peer contacts can be less than desirable. A Salt Lake City study showed that officers involved in shootings talk with their fellows 85 percent of the time.[20] Results show that fellow officers without proper training were reported to be of assistance in 59 percent of the cases, and in 41 percent of the cases surveyed, other officers were reported to be a major source of aggravation.[21]

Employees who experience short term crises need to be heard, need to have the opportunity to feel understood, and need to receive peer recognition of the extent of the problems they face. Peer counseling offers a means of effectively providing this support to employees who are under stress. With careful planning and implementation, an organization can provide a workable support network of peer counselors at a low cost to support fellow employees and the organization as a whole in resolving significant problems with a resulting increase in organizational efficiency and employee well-being.

About the Author

"Rusty" Capps has been an FBI Special Agent for fourteen years. His assignments include four years of criminal investigations in the FBI's San Francisco Office, and the last ten years in Los Angeles where he works foreign counter-intelligence matters. Prior to joining the FBI, Rusty served for eight years as a U.S. Army officer, reaching the grade of Major. Rusty has a B.A. from the University of Arizona, a Master's Degree in International Business, and is completing a Master's in Psychology. He has attended many military and Government schools, most recently completeing the State Department's Foreign Service Institute course on North Africa and the Middle East.

Footnotes

[1] Robert G. Phillips, Jr., "State and Local Law Enforcement Training Needs," *FBI Law Enforcement Bulletin*, Vol. 53, No. 8, August 1984, p. 9.

[2] Beth Ann Krier, "How Chief Gates Copes With Pressure at the Top," *Los Angeles Times*, February 4, 1982.

[3] James D. Sewell, "Police Stress," FBI Law Enforcement Bulletin, Vol. 50, No. 4, April 1981, p. 11.

[4] Roger L. Depue, "Turning Inward—The Police Officer Counselor," *FBI Law Enforcement Bulletin*, Vol. 48, No. 2, February 1979, p. 9.

[5] Eric Nielsen and Deen L. Eskridge, "Post Shooting Procedures: The Forgotten Officer," *Police Produce News*, July 1982, p. 41.

[6] D. Bracy, "Police Stress—The American Response," *England Police Journal*, Vol. 51, No. 3, July-September 1979, p. 263.

[7] Claudia Wallis, "Stress: Can We Cope?" *Time*, Vol. 121, No. 23, June 6, 1983, p. 54.

[8] Ibid., p. 54.

[9] Ibid.

[10] "Did 'Ya Hear About Harry?," *FBI Agent*, Vol. III, No. 2, Spring 1983, New Rochelle, NY, p. 4.

[11] Nels Klyver, "Peer Counseling for Police Personnel: A Dynamic Program in the Los Angeles Police Department," *The Police Chief*, Vol. L, No. 11, November 1983, p. 66.

[12] Jerry L. Powell, "Peer Counseling Guidelines," *LAPD Peer Counseling Newsletter*, Los Angeles, CA, November 2, 1982.

[13] Ibid., October 3, 1983.

[14] Supra note 11, p. 66.

[15] Joseph A. Durlak, "Comparative Effectiveness of Paraprofessional and Professional Helpers," *Psychological Bulletin*, Vol. 86, No. 1, 1979, p. 80.

[16] Supra note 11, p. 68.

[17] Supra note 2.

[18] Supra note 11, p. 68.

[19] Walter Lippert, "The Cost of Coming Out on Top—Emotional Responses to Surviving the Deadly Battle," *FBI Law Enforcement Bulletin*, Vol. 50, No. 12, December 1981, p. 9.

[20] Supra note 5.

[21] Supra note 5.

High-Risk Lifestyle: The Police Family

By Roger L. Depue

As I erased the chalkboard after the class, I noticed he was waiting to speak to me. I finished my chore and turned to face a well-built young man about 25 years of age. A fine looking law enforcement trainee, I thought.

"Yes, what can I do for you?" I said.

He smiled briefly and then his face turned serious as he said, "How am I going to tell my wife that this job comes first?"

"Pardon me?" I said.

"How am I going to tell my wife that this job must take precedence over everything else?" he continued. "I mean, how did you tell your wife?"

I paused, my eyes searching his face and finding only sincerity in it. I answered, "I've never had to tell her that."

Law enforcement work is a special kind of job. Sometimes it can be regarded as too special and it interferes with other important areas of human development and life satisfaction. One area often negatively affected by the police occupational lifestyle is the formation of a family life that is satisfying to all its members.

We will examine human development from three perspectives—individual, occupational, and familial—briefly review the literature regarding personal human development, introduce the concept of developmental tasks, and then turn to occupational development. The police occupation will be examined as it affects the personality of the police officer moving through the law enforcement career from police trainee to veteran officer. Finally, literature regarding the developmental process of family living will be examined.

The three areas of human development mentioned previously are important to life satisfaction but they can, and often do, conflict with one another. Overemphasis in one area can cause faulty development to occur in other areas. A balance must be established and maintained between each of the three areas in order to achieve a rewarding and satisfying life.

There has been a great deal written about the high incidence of marital discord and divorce among law enforcement officers. Marriage to a police officer involves coping with a difficult lifestyle. Police occupational development often seems to have an adverse impact on familial development. This unfortunate situation may be averted through knowledge of human development and the cultivation of interpersonal awareness and communication skills which tend to facilitate healthy development.

Background

A study of human nature reveals that man attempts to adapt to the environment by developing patterns of behavior that allow much of one's daily activities to become almost automatic. These patterns of behavior become the daily routine. To the extent that the environment changes, the old patterns of behavior are no longer appropriate for successful adaptation and new responses are experimented with. Eventually, new patterns of behavior which are more appropriate to living in the changed environment are developed and the daily routine changes.

This process of readaptation is stressful in that a change upsets the balance an individual has worked out between himself and the environment. As the amount of change increases, the individual must expend greater amounts of energy in order to find behavior that will reestablish the balance. Difficulty in adapting to significant change(s) over a period of centuries threatens the very survival of a species. On an individual level, failure to adapt to life change produces stress powerful enough to result in the deterioration of health, both mentally and physically.[1]

Human Development

Developmental psychology is the study of the ongoing formation of the human personality. The developmental process is usually described in terms of predictable stages of normal (based on norms) development. That is, development based on observations made by scientists studying large numbers of persons over long periods of time. Child development literature offers examples of established norms of growth, maturation, and development for infants. The normal infant is expected to creep, crawl, stand, and walk at predetermined periods of time (age levels) in the infancy growth cycle.[2] Any significant departure from the established norms is cause for concern to knowledgeable parents, teachers, and physicians. The developmental process should be monitored in order to identify potential problems in time to take corrective action so that continued development will not be adversely affected.

In the general field of psychology, Sigmund Freud was among the first to account for human behavior as being largely the result of early learning experiences during certain developmental stages that occur in accordance with a predetermined natural plan. In his psychoanalytic theory, he discussed the stages of psychosexual development as oral, anal, phallic, latency, and genital. Each stage of development was said to make new demands on the individual, to create new tasks which had to be dealt with successfully, and to arouse conflicts that had to be resolved before further growth and progress could take place.[3]

Today, the study of human development includes the entire lifespan of man. Among others, Erickson,[4] Havighurst,[5] Levinson,[6] and Sheehy[7] have identified stages, "seasons," or "passages" persons pass through on the lifelong journey from infancy to old age. Each development stage includes many predictable challenges, crises, and problems that must be met and resolved before further progress in life adaptation can continue.

Yale social psychologist Daniel Levinson says in his book, *The Seasons of a Man's Life,* that a man will experience at least three major life transition periods. He identifies them as early adult transition (ages 17-22 years), the midlife transition (ages 40-45 years), and the late adult transition (ages 60-65). Each transition period is a potential crisis and should be planned for, fully understood, and dealt with properly. A man must make appropriate adaptation responses to life changes or risk serious maladaptive consequences.[8]

Havighurst discusses the concept of developmental tasks.[9] Developmental tasks are adjustment problems tied to periods of life which must be successfully resolved before growth to more sophisticated levels of functioning can occur. Failure to resolve properly developmental tasks can, therefore, inhibit further development or cause "blind spots" to exist in certain areas of functioning. An example might be the need to learn appropriate intimate behavior between sexes during adolescence. Adolescents learning to embrace go through a trial and error period. There is desire, fear, uncertainty, awkwardness, groping, and misdirected aim. This unsophisticated condition is largely unnoticed by the adolescent partner, who is similarly confused. While the condition is appropriate for adolescents, it would certainly be inappropriate for a 30-year-old adult. An adult who does not have some level of sophistication involving skills for intimate contact with the opposite sex is socially impaired and may not find a partner with the patience and tolerance to afford the opportunity for this belated development. In other words, failure to develop certain life skills while in a particular growth phase can result in inappropriate functioning which adversely affects further development.

Occupational Development

Occupations also appear to have a pattern of development. For instance, there is the applicant phase, the recruit and training phase, the probationary period, the journeyman phase, the specialization, administrative advancement, or veteran phase, and the periods of preretirement, retirement, and postretirement. These stages of occupational development also have their attendant developmental tasks and conflicts. They, too, must be recognized and dealt with for successful adjustment to life circumstances.

In law enforcement, the applicant is often a person who views the job in an idealistic and "romantic" way. The fictionalized "super cop" image fostered by the media has frequently contributed to the occupational interest of this jobseeker.

Screening and selection procedures also serve to give the recruit officer a feeling of joining a specially chosen and somewhat elite group of persons.

The training period can be likened to the beginning of an aculturation process. The trainee begins to attach to and identify with the police culture.

Dr. Martin Reiser, Los Angeles Police Department psychologist, explains it as follows:

> "The recruit's concept of himself undergoes some modification as those attributes in his value system change along with his new identification as a police officer. He may see himself as opposed to and disliking people and behavior that were previously conflict free."[10]

The homogeneity of the peer group, the mutual expectations of the job, and the uniformity of standards contribute to the formation of an occupational personality. The young police officer actually looks, acts, and feels different from other members of society.

During the probationary period, the officer works hard to prove competence and gain acceptance within the group. He experiences "shock" at trying to provide services, maintain order, and enforce laws among persons who often hate and despise what police work represents. The officer becomes more and more defensive. It is a difficult time, requiring much new learning.

In the next stage the officer develops a tough exterior to help cope with the threats of abuse and the personal danger of the working environment. Reiser refers to this toughening process as the "John Wayne Syndrome."[11] It impacts both male and female officers and involves a cool authoritative demeanor and over-control of emotion. This behavioral syndrome lasts for several years. The officer spends long hours on the job, uses police jargon, associates with police types, and is suspicious and critical of nonpolice people. Niederhoffer examined the changes which occur in police personality from idealism to cynicism over a period of years, noting that cynicism peaks at about the eighth year of service.[12]

The journeyman phase is next. The officer begins to settle down and mellow. The years of experience have provided poise and self-confidence so the job can be accomplished in a more relaxed and comfortable manner.[13] It is at this developmental stage that serious career decisions are made. These decisions lead to a continuation in the present assignment as a veteran patrol officer, the development of a specialization (detective, training, police community relations work, etc.), or to administrative advancement.

The retirement periods include dealing with preretirement, retirement, and postretirement developmental tasks. It is a time of "mustering out" of the brotherhood and rejoining the general society. It is often an unsettling time, involving a great change in lifestyle.

Familial Development

As in the studies of personal human development and occupational development, social scientists studying families have also identified a developmental process in the life cycle of the family. To start a family is to start a new organization. The partners bring with them hopes, fears, desires, expectations, habits, and values from the families of origin. It is very important for the partners to take the necessary steps early in the relationship to solve problems arising from differing personal histories and move toward a mutually satisfying lifestyle.

Noted family therapist Salvador Minuchin discusses the family as follows:

> "The family is a social unit that faces a series of developmental tasks. These differ along the parameters of cultural differences, but they have universal roots."[14]

Minuchin says that every family must solve the problems of relating to one another, raising children, dealing with the in-laws, and coping with the outside world. To make life together possible, a new couple must participate in a series of negotiations to arrive at necessary compromises. In an effort to arrive at mutual accommodation, negotiations are necessary to establish routines for such activities as going to bed, getting up, eating meals, being naked, achieving sexual satisfaction, "going out," and sharing such things as the bathroom, television, and the Sunday morning comics.[15]

Minuchin points out that each marriage partner must separate from the family of origin and establish a new satisfying relationship with the other partner. They must develop "patterned transactions"—ways in which one partner monitors and triggers behavior in the other. He refers to these transactional patterns as a "web of complementary demands."[16]

It is important to note that if these developmental tasks are not successfully resolved, progress toward mutual accommodation can be impaired and development of a deeper relationship inhibited. Just as with the adolescent who does not have successful experiences in building relationships with members of the opposite sex and is later "ill-at-ease" in their presence, so too is the marriage partner who has not worked out a system for resolving disagreements over lifestyle and is later uncomfortable and unable to move toward satisfaction of personal desires.

In his book, *Families and Family Therapy,* Minuchin gives an example of a young couple who delayed addressing some developmental tasks of early marriage because the male partner was a full-time college student and did not have the time to learn to be a husband and father. When he graduated from college, he was literally a misfit in his family roles. He had to attempt to learn what he had missed. He had to develop the patterned transactions leading to his own satisfaction, the satisfaction of his spouse, and each of his children. He had to struggle to learn that communicative behavior which he could have "naturally" learned at the appropriate time and phase of life.[17]

The idea of balance also enters into theories of family development. Dr. Murry Bowen, a pioneer in family therapy, has characterized the family as a system. Bowen states that "any relationship with balancing forces and counterforces in constant operation is a system."[18]

Family systems theory is a special kind of applied psychology that deals with intimate relationships. It examines the roles of the individual family members, the context, rules, alliances, and frequently traces family history and development back through several generations.

When it is operating in balance, the family represents one of man's most efficient methods for achieving satisfaction of human needs and desires. When the balance is upset, life can become miserable.

Entering police work imposes a significant change of environment for the officer and his family. The police officer is removed from the mainstream of American life. The uniform sets the officer apart from other members of society, and the nature of the work is unlike that of any other occupation. The officer is often awake while others are asleep, at work while others are at play, and at home while others are traveling on a holiday.

The occupational lifestyle all too frequently upsets the balance of family life. The new spouse of the officer has expectations of what married life will be like. These expectations are usually based on the lifestyle of an "ordinary" American family. The farther reality deviates from the expected, the greater the strain on the adjustment mechanisms.

Dr. Bowen puts it this way:

"When anxiety increases and remains chronic for a certain period, the organism develops tension, either within itself or in the relationship system, and the tension results in symptoms or dysfunction or sickness."[19]

The Family vs. The Job

When the developmental process of the law enforcement occupation is coupled with that of the family, severe strain can result, especially during the early stages of each. In other words, trouble can be expected in the relationship of the recently married "rookie" police officer. At the same time the job is making the greatest demands and exerting the most influence on the new officer, the marriage is requiring the most attention and positive efforts for relationship building.

Like the college student in Minuchin's example who was dominated by his student role, a police officer can be dominated by the occupational role. Dr. Minuchin points out that following marriage, the new couple must resolve a variety of developmental tasks leading to "mutual accommodation." For instance, he says, "Decisions must be reached as to how the demands of the outside world will be allowed to intrude on the life of the new family."[20]

Police wife Pat James described how the job of her husband became part of her married life:

"One of the first revelations was that I was involved from the very start in a triangle, a three-sided romance. My rival was, is, and apparently always will be my husband's work."[21]

This statement characterizes the feelings of many wives of police officers. Elaine Niederhoffer, co-author of *The Police Family: From Station House to Ranch House,* reiterates the feeling by entitling the first chapter of her book, "The Police Occupation: A Jealous Mistress."[22]

When one examines this view of the police officer's job from the viewpoint of family systems theory, it takes on rather weighty importance. When an occupation is viewed as being such an integral part of the family, there exists the very real possibility that the occupation will become part of a triangle.

Dr. Bowen defines a triangle as "a three-person emotional configuration. . . ."[23] It is the smallest stable relationship system.

Dr. Bowen explains it:

"In periods of calm, the triangle is made up of a comfortably close twosome and less comfortable outsider. The twosome works to preserve the togetherness, lest one become uncomfortable and form a better togetherness elsewhere. The outsider seeks to form a togetherness with one of the twosome. . . ."[24]

The core problem in the relationship system is called fusion. Fusion indicates a blurring of self-boundaries, the merging of self and other, the loss of individual identity. Normally, if the pull for togetherness becomes too strong, and it threatens to usurp individuality, there is a counteractive pull away.

Family therapists Elizabeth A. Carter and Monica McGoldrick Orfanidis explain triangling as follows:

"Few people can relate personally for very long before running into some issue in their relationship that makes one or both anxious, at which point it is automatic to triangle in a third person or thing as a way of diverting the anxiety in the relationship of the twosome. It is dysfunctional in the sense that it offers stabilization through diversion, rather than through resolution of the issue in the twosome's relationship. Thus a couple under stress may focus on a child whose misbehavior gives them something to come together on in mutual concern. Repeated over time, triangling will become a chronic dysfunctional pattern preventing resolution of differences in the marriage and making one

or more of the three vulnerable to physical or emotional symptoms, because stabilization with dysfunction, although problematic, is experienced as preferable to change."[25]

Fogarty describes triangles as "the building blocks of the immature family." It is the effort to project the problem in a relationship outside and onto another person or thing.[26]

Carter and Orfanidis talk about detriangling as "the process whereby one of these three frees himself from the enmeshment of the three and develops separate person-to-person relationships with each of the other two."[27]

Applied to the police occupation, this means that a job viewed with such importance may be treated like a person by the officer and like a scapegoat by the spouse. Friction with the spouse may move the officer closer to the job as a source of satisfaction and pleasure. The same friction may cause the spouse to project the blame onto the occupation instead of confronting the officer partner.

Neither action does anything to address the real problem of the faulty family relationship. The unresolved conflicts build toward symptom formation and dysfunction within the system. Detriangling is necessary. The fusion must be broken up and person-to-person relations reestablished.

All families experience conflict. The families affording the greatest satisfaction to their members have found ways to resolve successfully the serious conflicts. The process of resolving conflict involves dealing with developmental tasks which occur at various stages in the relationship so that progress toward greater satisfaction (Minuchin's mutual accommodation) can be accomplished. Until developmental tasks are dealt with, the relationship remains at a premature level of development. It is like the child who never learns to talk. Language is essential to most areas of further social development and without this communicative skill the person cannot proceed to higher levels of human functioning.

In addition, the police occupation imposes a nontraditional lifestyle on family members. To cope with the stress of a different lifestyle, it is necessary that a communication process be established that will allow negotiation of the many inevitable conflicts and lead toward mutual accommodation.

Family therapists Bandler, Grinder, and Satir have divided disturbed family relationships into two conceptual areas—content and process. Content involves the actual problems that exist in the family; process is how the family attempts to deal with the problems. Process which is independent of content "focuses on the patterns of coping within the family system, irrespective of the specific problems found within the family."[28]

Bandler, Grinder, and Satir's "model of family therapy is designed to assist the family in coping effectively at the process level."[29] Assisting family members in having new choices at the process level in any area of content will generalize naturally to other areas of their experience.

In the dysfunctional (police) family, it is absolutely necessary to improve the process of communication by which conflict is resolved and mutual satisfaction is accomplished. Miller, Nunnally, and Wackman discuss a style of communication to accomplish these ends. This style involves learning skills for expressing one's intention to deal with an issue openly and directly by setting forth a procedure for discussion, by being in contact with accepting and disclosing one's self-awareness, by trying to understand and value the partner's self-awareness, and by taking responsible action to improve communication.[30]

That conclusion was also reached by Nancy Welch Maynard and Peter W. Maynard of the University of Rhode Island. The Maynards have conducted research on police family stress at the Minnesota Family Study Center and were responsible for instituting a communication training program in the police academy. "Mindful of the fact that divorce among police couples is soaring, officials of the Rhode Island Municipal Police Academy initiated offering the Minnesota couple communication program to police couples as a preventive measure."[31]

Since the police family lifestyle is atypical, it is probable that there will be more adjustment necessary for family members and more areas of conflict to resolve. If, during the early years in the relationship, a process for dealing with conflict is not maturely developed, anxiety and discomfort mount. The parties of the relationship must work out developmental tasks which were not addressed at an earlier, more appropriate time. They must work out a negotiation process. This is very

difficult to do, but the alternative is likely to be a life of frustration and/or separation.

Balanced Development

A balance must be maintained between the three areas of human development. Each area can interfere with the other. For instance (as we saw in the Minuchin example) personal development, such as pursuing a college degree, can sometimes detract from occupational and/or familial growth. We have all observed instances where a student is so concerned with studies that occupational performance and familial relationships deteriorate. For such a person, everything must revolve around school attendance. Many police officers are also attending college classes, and it is not uncommon to hear their supervisors question their dedication to the job and spouses question their dedication to the family.

Extreme dedication to the family can also serve to upset the development balance. An example of family domination might be an individual who must call the spouse from work many times a day. There is usually a ritual of endearments recited to assure each other that the family relationship is foremost. The individual who cannot even temporarily separate from the family influence is often inhibited from personal growth and/or occupational development. Business travel or working overtime is out of the question. During any temporary separation, the telephone line becomes the umbilical cord. In this relationship, occasionally stopping for coffee or a social drink after work is unthought of by one spouse and is positive proof to the other that such a person cannot love his or her family.

From the occupational standpoint, we have all seen the person who is totally absorbed in the job. Personal growth is equated with occupational growth. Family seems to exist only to support this person in the pursuit of occupational goals. This overemphasis of the occupation leads to underemphasis on nonoccupational personal growth and family life. For example, such persons may realize too late in life that they have always wanted to learn to play a musical instrument but somehow never had the time to do it. Worse yet, they may realize that they barely know family members and can reflect on few meaningful family memories.

Conclusion

Healthy human development requires balance. None of the areas of development can be "sacrificed" for the sake of the others—growth must occur in each area.

Most police families run the risk of occupational domination, especially during the early years of the relationship. Family development and personal development unrelated to the job are often relegated to the "back burner" by the officer. Developmental tasks in these areas are not addressed and negotiations leading to a lifestyle providing satisfaction to each family member are not accomplished.

In response to the young officer who asked how he should explain to his wife that the job must take precedence over anything else, we must answer, "Yes, the job is an extremely important one, but balance is even more important." Human beings are multidimensional and must grow in a variety of ways to attain life satisfaction. A healthy family relationship is a great source of support during times of stress. The law enforcement occupation is a stressful job and a good police officer must take care to protect and cultivate this source of strength. The job does not take precedence over the family. The job takes its place in the total balanced developmental scheme. If we are to speak of precedence at all, it is balanced growth that takes precedence over lopsided development.

About the Author

Special Agent Roger L. Depue serves as chief of Behavioral Sciences at the FBI Academy, Quantico, Virginia. He is the developer of the National Center for the Analysis of Violent Crime (NCAVC), a national clearinghouse for unsolved violent crimes, and serves as its administrator. He holds a Bachelor of Science Degree in psychology from Central Michigan University, a master's degree in the Administration of Justice, and a Ph.D. in Counseling and Development from The American University. Dr. Depue has been an adjunct faculty member for the University of Virginia for 14 years teaching courses in the disciplines of psychology and sociology. His writings on law enforcement topics have been published internationally. He is also a former Chief of Police and a county juvenile officer.

Footnotes

[1] B.S. Dohrenwend and B.P. Dohrenwend, *Stressful Life Events: Their Nature and Effects* (New York: John Wiley and Sons, Inc., 1974), p. 68.

[2] Elizabeth B. Hurlock, *Child Development*, 4th ed. (New York: McGraw-Hill, Inc., 1964), p. 173.

[3] J.C. Coleman, *Abnormal Psychology and Modern Life*, 5th ed. (Glenview, Ill.: Scott, Foresman and Company, 1976), p. 56.

[4] Erik H. Erikson, *Childhood and Society* (New York: W.H. Norton and Company, Inc., 1963), p. 273.

[5] R.J. Havighurst, "Social and Developmental Psychology: Trends Influencing the Future of Counseling," *The Personnel and Guidance Journal*, January 1980, Vol. 58, No. 5, pp. 326-333.

[6] D.J. Levinson with C.N. Darrow, E.B. Klein, M.H. Levinson, and B.McKee, *The Seasons of a Man's Life* (New York: Alfred A. Knopf, Inc., 1978).

[7] G. Sheehy, *Passages: Predictable Crises in Adult Life* (New York: Bantam Books Edition, 1977).

[8] Levinson, p. 20.

[9] Havighurst, pp. 328-333.

[10] M. Reiser, *Practical Psychology for Police Officers* (Springfield, Ill.: Charles C. Thomas, 1973), p. 8.

[11] Ibid., p. 17.

[12] Arthur Niederhoffer, *Behind the Shield: The Police in Urban Society* (New York: Doubleday Anchor, 1969), p. 239.

[13] Reiser, p. 15.

[14] S. Minuchin, *Families and Family Therapy* (Cambridge, Mass.: Harvard University Press, 1974), p. 16.

[15] Ibid., p. 17.

[16] Ibid., p. 17.

[17] Ibid., pp. 18-45.

[18] M. Bowen, "Theory in the Practice of Psychotherapy," *Family Therapy: Theory and Practice,* ed. P.J. Guerin (New York: Gardner Press, Inc., 1976), p. 62.

[19] Ibid., p. 65

[20] Minuchin, p. 17.

[21] P. James and M. Nelson, "The Police Family: A Wife's Eye View," *FBI Law Enforcement Bulletin,* November 1975, pp. 12-15.

[22] A. Niederhoffer and E. Niederhoffer, *The Police Family: From Station House to Ranch House* (Lexington, Mass.: D.C. Heath and Company, 1978), p. 1.

[23] Bowen, p. 75.

[24] Ibid., p. 76.

[25] E.A. Carter and M.M. Orfanidis, "Family Therapy with One Person and the Family Therapist's Own Family," *Family Therapy: Theory and Practice,* ed. P.J. Guerin (New York: Gardner Press, Inc. 1976), p. 197.

[26] T.F. Fogarty, "Marital Crisis," in *Family Therapy: Theory and Practice*, ed. P.J. Guerin (New York: Gardner Press, Inc., 1976), p. 331.

[27] Carter, p. 197.

[28] R. Bandler, J. Grinder, and V. Satir, *Changing With Families: A Book About Further Education for Being Human* (Palo Alto, Calif.: Science and Behavior Books, Inc., 1976), p. 96.

[29] Ibid., p. 97.

[30] S. Miller, E.W. Nunnelly, and D.B. Wackman, *Alive and Aware: How to Improve Your Relationships Through Better Communication* (Minneapolis, Minn.: Interpersonal Communications Program, Inc., 1975), p. 21.

[31] P.E. Maynard and N.W. Maynard, "Preventing Family Stress Through Couples Communication Training," *The Police Chief,* February 1980.

Retirement: Is It the End or the Beginning?

By Thomas Ammann
and
Paul Meyer

From recruit classes through various inservice training programs, police agencies place heavy emphasis on developing and maintaining their officers' proficiency in decisonmaking. However, it seems the agency often overlooks training at a very important point in an officer's career—RETIREMENT.

Recently, the Cincinnati Police Division was informed that a revised pension system for the State of Ohio would soon be implemented. This change would allow police officers to retire at age 48 rather than the previous 52 years of age.

A review of the division's personnel records indicated that of 939 sworn officers, 106 would be eligible to retire under the new pension system. Realizing the potentially large number of police officers facing retirement, a brainstorming session was conducted by the Academy's staff to formulate a framework for a preretirement seminar.

Program Formulation

A survey of numerous police agencies revealed few programs for the potential retiree. The private sector was surveyed, and it was discovered that the more progressive corporations conduct retirement programs on a limited basis.

A comprehensive program needed to be designed to assist the potential retiree. Areas to be covered in the program would include physical and psychological trauma associated with retirement, financial advice, need for wills and/or trusts, and second career orientation, as well as an explanation of the new system's benefits.

As the planning progressed, input was solicited from the Great Oaks Vocational School District of the State of Ohio, which was offering a retirement program. The Cincinnati Police Division's pension system liaison officer was also contacted for his ideas. After considerable discussion, a 12-hour pre-retirement seminar was formulated. It would be offered on an off-duty status three successive Wednesday nights, 4 hours each night, to any sworn member of the police division contemplating retirement within the next year.

The Police Academy distributed questionnaires throughout the division inquiring as to whether personnel were interested in attending a preretirement seminar and whether spouses could accompany them. (This was considered an essential part of the program, since emotional and marital problems can result from retirement.) When the questionnaires were returned and the results tabulated, the figures revealed that out of 106 potential retirees, 37 sworn members and 18 spouses would attend.

As planning for the program progressed, it became apparent that retirement is often associated with a feeling of rejection and diminution of personal worth. One afternoon, while completing the course outline, an officer called the Academy concerning a situation unrelated to the retirement seminar. After several minutes, discussion turned toward the proposed program. When asked why he decided not to attend the seminar, the officer offered several reasons. It appeared, however, that the real reason was his refusal to accept the fact he was old enough to retire. His parting comment was, "I'm too young to retire."

Program Content

The initial 4-hour segment of the seminar addressed the benefits of the recently revised pension system, as well as second career opportunities. The lecturer on pension system benefits was a police specialist who had served on the board of the Police and Firemen's Disability Pension Fund at local and State levels for over 20 years. A retired vice president of a large financial institution then discussed

State-funded training programs and counseling available for those seeking a new career. He also discussed his personal adjustment to a second career.

The second evening consisted of the more technical monetary decisions facing the potential retiree—wills, trusts, and investments. An attorney, and long-time instructor at the University of Cincinnati, explained the advantage of having a current will. He also presented an informative session concerning the advantages of trusts. During the final session for the evening, an investment adviser from a local bank discussed the various options available when considering stocks, bonds, and retirement accounts, together with their effect on retirement income.

The final evening was divided into three parts—insurance, mental health, and physical health. The vice president of a local insurance company discussed using insurance to advantage after retirement. The next instructor was a psychiatrist who delved into the mental and emotional health of both the retiree and his spouse during the retirement years. He pointed out that the potential increase in time spent together can be a source of marital friction and stressed the need for outside hobbies and interests to occupy the newly acquired leisure time. The final portion of the evening, presented by a field representative fitness expert of the Cincinnati Recreation Commission, addressed the need for continued physical fitness. Health problems related to the aging process were specifically discussed.

Midway through the program, several participants urged the Police Academy to consider asking a retired officer to share his view of retirement. As a result, on the final evening, a former sergeant agreed to an informal exchange on the subject.

As is the case with many of the programs presented by the Police Academy, the retirement seminar was recorded on 1/2-inch reel-to-reel video tape. The purpose of taping the program was twofold: to assist the Academy staff in improving future programs and to provide a makeup class for anyone who may have missed a session. The tapes are available in the Academy library for the convenience of the participants.

Evaluation

Each program presented at the Cincinnati Police Academy is evaluated by the attendees. Everyone is requested to rate the course on a scale of one (lowest) to five (highest). In addition to soliciting a numerical score, the evaluation forms provide space for additional comments and suggestions. This program was rated an overall 4.73.

Comments offered ranged from "an excellent program, very motivating and long overdue," to "all speakers deserve the highest praise for their presentations."

The preretirement seminar illustrated to the potential retiree that even beyond his active service, the police division is genuinely interested in his well-being. It also marked the first time that police officers and their spouses attended training classes together at the Academy.

The written evaluations and informal exchanges among the seminar participants, instructors, and Academy staff demonstrated the program's value. Consequently, the seminar will be offered on an annual basis in the future.

Conclusion

Thoughts of career development, particularly in law enforcement, involve consideration of promotions, transfers, details, and assignments. The critiques of this preretirement seminar have fostered the belief that retirement may be the most ignored phase of career development.

The Cincinnati Police Academy strongly urges both public and private sectors to consider expanding the concept of career development to include preparation for retirement. As one of the officer's wives stated in her evaluation, "This (seminar) was a very noble gesture on the part of the Police Division. My husband and I looked at retirement with reservation; now we look at it not as the end of a career, but the start of a new and different lifestyle."

About the Authors

Lt. Colonel Thomas Ammann is an Assistant Police Chief with the Cincinnati Police Division and is currently Commander of the Personnel Resources Bureau. Colonel Ammann is an Adjunct Professor at the University of Cincinnati and has taught Police Administration at that University. He also teaches report writing and organization/management courses at the Cincinnati Police Academy.

Colonel Ammann holds an A.S. in Police Science and a B.S. in Criminal Justice from the University of Cincinnati and a Master of Business Administration from Xavier University. He has authored numerous magazine articles on law enforcement.

Paul G. Meyer is a Police Specialist with the Cincinnati Police Division and is currently assigned as a records collator. Prior assignments include Research and Planning, Criminal Justice Section and the Police Academy. While at the Police Academy, Specialist Meyer conducted recruit training, inservice training for veteran officers, as well as a number of programs for civilian personnel. At present, he is actively involved in the training of private security personnel in the greater Cincinnati area. Specialist Meyer holds an A.S. in Police Science and a B.S. in Education from the University of Cincinnati, and a M.Ed. from Xavier University.

Police and Personnel — A Continuum

By Thomas J. Deakin

Police service in America was, and is today, exactly that—a service.

Police forces in this country developed on the London model of police as a service that was to be ". . .in tune with the people, understanding the people, and drawing its strength from the people."[1] This new police service was to replace the military for society's necessary function of order control.

Use of the military for order control had been found wanting in relation to Anglo-Saxon concepts of humanity that were beginning to develop early in the 19th century. Thus, London police personnel were deliberately civilian in nature, in contrast to the military origins and orientation of continental police at that time.

Today, American police are reinforcing the concept of the civilian nature of the police over the military model. Police today recognize the individual officer's responsibility to do more than just follow orders. The co-editor of this book, Special Agent Steve Gladis, had the idea of compiling for the first time in a single volume the cooperative efforts of *FBI Law Enforcement Bulletin* contributors on the important subject of police personnel. The *Bulletin* has long been a training tool for police personnel, with it contributions from all elements of the criminal justice field, including academics, who have also contributed to this volume.

The *Bulletin* is also an important historical record of developments in policing since the 1930's. Over a decade as editor of the *Bulletin* has allowed me a particular perspective on the police personnel continuum: where we have been, where we are today, and where I believe we are headed in the next century.

Where We Have Been

In historical terms, in the century since the Civil War American policing has evolved from being a tool of corrupt ward politicians—as it became soon after its founding in this country, and a device to implement immigration's upward social mobility—to an efficient service with the beginnings of professional stature. At first, this was due to the influence of the Progressive Movement on local governments, but most of the movement toward professionalism has been through the leadership of the law enforcement community itself. Through the efforts of the personnel in policing, the law enforcement community has literally pulled itself up by its own bootstraps.

We see a continuum for police personnel, beginning with police pioneer August Vollmer, chief of police in Berkeley, California, who in 1919, was the first proponent of the "new policeman," the police officer who would "do good solid, constructive social service."[2] At the turn of the century, through the 1920's, policing was affected by the "good government" forces of the Progressive Era. In the 1930's, policing and its personnel adopted a new model: J. Edgar Hoover's FBI and an emphasis on crime fighting by college graduates, a new concept in the investigation of crime.

The aftermath of World War II resurrected the military model of policing that had been prevalent after the first world war. As a result new police theorists, such as O.W. Wilson and Los Angeles chief of police William Parker, promulgated the concept of firm executive control.

Chief Parker, for example, cleaned up the Los Angeles Police Department, and in the 1950s it became the exemplar of "efficient" policing, with a high percentage of World War II vets in the ranks. The Los Angeles police represented the times when police officers became encapsulated in their patrol cars, lost contact with the community, and became, in stern demeanor, almost militaristic. Patrick V. Murphy, who rose through the ranks of the New York City Police Department to become police commissioner of this nation's largest depart- ment, once noted that the Los Angeles police didn't know how to smile.[3]

Across the nation, this milieu of treating police officers as soldiers or automatons, rather than as people, along with economic factors, contributed to the greatest police personnel problem in the 1960's: corruption. Widespread dishonesty among police personnel, including even burglary rings of police officers, placed corruption foremost in the minds of police executives in that decade.

In fact, corruption, along with the urban rioting in the late 1960's, led to the appointment of an FBI field manager as chief of police in Kansas City.[4] That appointment, and the formation of the Police Foundation—which itself came about because of policing's inability to perform its historic role of order maintenance—sparked a new renaissance in policing, with an emphasis on personnel, both managerial and rank and file.

Where We Are Now

Today's era of policing is marked first, by the willingness of police personnel to conduct experiments in the social sciences to evaluate the various functions of policing, and their effects on both the public and police personnel. At the same time, our society has changed from placing an emphasis on protection of property rights to a new concern with human and individual rights. Even the rights and responsibilities of police personnel are now being examined. Policing has thus followed society's lead, as it should in a democracy.

Carefully planned social science experiments by police departments, with the cooperation of the academic staff of the Police Foundation, have challenged some of the basic assumptions of policing in the late 1960's and 1970's. The Kansas City patrol experiment, begun when Clarence Kelley was chief of police in that city, showed that preventive motor patrol was not the answer to crime control. As the decade of the 1960's progressed, experiments were broadened to include measurement of the effects of the experiments not only on the community, but on police personnel.

For example, the Newark foot patrol experiment showed that foot patrol did not reduce crime, as preventive patrol hadn't either, but did "measurably

and significantly affect citizens' feeling of safety and mobility in their neighborhoods." As important, this experiment measured the attitudes and performance of foot and motor patrol officers. "Foot patrol officers are more satisfied with police work... they have a more benign view of citizens, a lower absenteeism record, and a more community-oriented view of the police function."[5]

Where We Are Going

Today and into the next century, we are finally returning to the premises on which the London police were founded: that the police service was to be, ". . . in tune with the people, understanding the people, and drawing its strength from the people." This concept has taken the form of community policing, law enforcement's answer to the serious challenges that have been made to patrol practices. Policing today is involving the community's citizens in crime control and prevention to a degree unprecedented in America's past.

Community policing can, and does, include establishing neighborhood storefront police stations, decentralized team policing, crime prevention or resistance programs, neighborhood watches, "Crime Stopper" media reward strategies, and other innovative programs. These are designed to involve the whole of the citizenry in police efforts to improve the quality of life in our communities through both order control and law enforcement by police personnel.

Community policing will affect police personnel in two ways: first, it helps prevent the boredom of routine motor patrol that contributes to personnel burnout. Second, this new mode of policing will require higher caliber, and better educated, personnel who can meet the variety of challenges presented by this type of policing.

Other elements of the criminal justice community have joined with police personnel in researching workable strategies to improve policing through the control of crime and disorder. The Police Executive Research Forum (formed by Patrick Murphy and the Police Foundation to include college-educated police executives of the largest departments in this country), the Justice Department's National Institute of Justice, and the FBI have all contributed to this effort to find answers. The FBI's National

Center for the Analysis of Violent Crime, for example, is a cooperative effort with local police personnel to solve crimes involving violence with trans-jurisdictional aspects, through use of profiling and computerization of the investigative process.

Also of significance to police personnel is the recent move toward accreditation of police agencies. Begun by the International Association of Chiefs of Police, the National Sheriffs Association, the National Organization of Black Law Enforcement Officers, and the Police Executive Research Forum, the two-year-long voluntary accreditation process began in the fall of 1983. Just four years later, some 51 police agencies had been accredited and another 560 were in the process of complying with the several hundred standards set by the Accreditation Commission.

This process meets a need where an individual State does not have minimum standards for law enforcement personnel, or the standards, in the view of the police organizations involved in the accreditation process, are not sufficient. We will see, in our increasingly mobile society, that police agencies that are accredited (other factors being essentially equal) will attract the best recruits—the long-term basis of a good department.

These, then, are the routes police are taking at the end of the 20th century: (1) community policing, with its variety of strategies adaptable to different communities or even neighborhoods, but always involving the citizenry of the community closely with police personnel; (2) continued research efforts by the law enforcement community on developing crime problems and on the policing process; and (3) accreditation to insure that communities have law enforcement agencies and personnel who can meet new challenges of the 21st century.

The editors of this work hope that this compilation of articles on personnel from the *FBI Law Enforcement Bulletin* has helped police mana- gers to face the personnel challenges that the changing nature of police professionalism will un- doubtedly present in the next century.

About the Author

Special Agent Thomas J. Deakin, J.D., former Editor of the FBI Law Enforcement Bulletin (LEB), *retired in December, 1988, from the FBI after 28 years of service. A graduate of Washington University School of Law in St. Louis, and a former police officer, he was the Editor of the* LEB *for over 11 years, which is the longest period served by an editor in the history of the publication. Tom has also used his knowledge and expertise to write* Police Professionalism: The Renaissance of American Law Enforcement, *published in 1988 by Charles C. Thomas. His book is a history of police professionalism and has made a major contribution to the law enforcement profession. Currently, Tom is teaching the criminal justice courses at American University.*

Endnotes

[1] Critchley, T.A., *A History of Police in England and Wales* (Montclair, N.J.: Constable & Co. Ltd., 1967, reprinted 1972 Patterson Smith), p. 52.

[2] Vollmer, August, "The Policeman as a Social Worker," *The Policeman's News* (August 1919), 6:12.

[3] Murphy, Patrick V., *Commissioner: A View From the Top of American Law Enforcement* (New York, N.Y.: Simon and Schuster, 1977), p. 40.

[4] Kelley, Clarence M., *Kelley, The Story of an FBI Director* (New York, N.Y.: Andrews, McMeal & Parker, 1987), p. 69.

[5] Police Foundation, *The Newark Foot Patrol Experiment* (Washington, D.C.: Police Foundation, 1981), pp. iii, 109.

PART TWO

RESOURCE MATERIALS

CHAPTER V

Training and Development Forms and Checklists

Demographic and Biographical Data

Participant Information

1. _____
       Last Name   *First Name*   *What You Like To Be Called*

2. Birthday: _____   _____
               Month   *Day*

3. When did you join this organization?   _____   _____
                                       Month   *Year*

4. What is your present Position/Title?_____

5. When did you take on this title?   _____   _____
                               Month   *Year*

6. List other positions in which you performed skills/duties similar to those you will study in this program?

POSITION   **SKILL**

_____   _____

_____   _____

_____   _____

7. About the skills/concepts you expect to acquire in this program:

    A. I perform them now.   YES   NO
    B. I expect to perform them within the next month   YES   NO
    C. The percent of my time which is/will be spent doing this is   _____%
    D. If "NO" is your answer to A or B, what is your understanding about the
        reason you are attending this program?

8. Did you discuss the program objectives and the reasons for your participation
    with your immediate supervisor/manager?   YES   NO

9. What other related personal growth goals would you like to pursue during this program?

10. What two or three adjectives could you use to show that this program had been a success *for you*?

_____   _____   _____

11. What adjectives would best describe your feeling when you learned you would attend this program?

_____   _____   _____

12. What would you like us to know about your education and previous training?

13. List any special problems which your instructors should know about.

Feelings About Being Enrolled

How Were You Enrolled?

Take just a couple of minutes to answer these questions by check mark, short answer or YES/NO responses.

1. My organization is PROFIT-MAKING_____ GOVERNMENTAL_____ ACADEMIC_____
   NON-PROFIT ASSOCIATION _____

   My department is PRODUCTION_____ SALES_____ ADMINISTRATION_____ PERSONNEL_____
   OTHER (SPECIFY)_____

2. I myself made the decision to attend this training.   YES   NO

3. If notified to attend, I was told by:
   My immediate boss_____ Someone higher on my chain of command_____ The Training Department_____

   If "None of the above," please specify: _____

   I was notified in writing_____ By an oral message_____

   The notification reached me about _____ days OR _____ weeks before the first day of training.

4. If YES or NO won't quite tell the story, use the COMMENTS column at the right.

   Before I left work to attend this training, my boss:

                                                                    COMMENTS

   Explained why I was attending.   YES   NO   _____

   Explained what I was supposed to learn
   while I am here.   YES   NO   _____

   Explained how I'd apply the learning to
   my work after I return.   YES   NO   _____

   Related my attendance to a development plan,
   career path or personal performance problem.   YES   NO   _____

   If you answered YES, encircle the correct reason.

5. The way I was notified made me feel: (Check ALL applicable answers)
   Happy____ Honored____ Eager to Learn____   That I was expected to work hard while here____
   Anxious____ Punished____ Negative____   That I was expected to learn something____
                                                   That I had earned some rest and recreation____
   Other: (Specify)   That I'm supposed to do things differently in future____

6. As I perceive it, I was ASKED TO ATTEND____ TOLD TO ATTEND____ ASKED IF I WISHED TO
   ATTEND ____
   I myself ASKED TO ATTEND____, and I found it was EASY____ DIFFICULT ____ to get approval.

HRD Press, 22 Amherst Rd., Amherst, MA 01002. 1-800-822-2801

Viewpoints About Training Tasks

Use the numbers at the left to show your estimate of the importance of the training tasks listed at the center of the page.

> *Use the number 5 to indicate "Very Important."*
> *Let the number 4 show the task to be "Quite Important."*
> *Use the number 3 to indicate tasks of "Medium Significance."*
> *Let the number 2 indicate tasks of "Necessary but Minor" impact,*
> *And the number 1 indicates your opinion that tasks are of "No Importance."*

Do not use the column at the right of the page until later.

IMPORTANCE						PREFERENCE				
5	4	3	2	1	Analyze performance problems and counsel line and staff personnel about training activities.	5	4	3	2	1
5	4	3	2	1	Do a task analysis, outlining the detailed steps for performing a task.	5	4	3	2	1
5	4	3	2	1	Develop training programs to meet the task requirements.	5	4	3	2	1
5	4	3	2	1	Secure support for the training function and its programs.	5	4	3	2	1
5	4	3	2	1	Maintain ongoing relationships with the users of training services.	5	4	3	2	1
5	4	3	2	1	Arrange facilities, schedule programs, keep things running smoothly.	5	4	3	2	1
5	4	3	2	1	Communicate ideas in classroom or in conference settings.	5	4	3	2	1
5	4	3	2	1	Stimulate and lead group interaction in classes and conferences.	5	4	3	2	1
5	4	3	2	1	Detect and respond to hidden agendas in individuals, groups and organizations.	5	4	3	2	1
5	4	3	2	1	Apply the human resource development findings of psychologists and scholars.	5	4	3	2	1
5	4	3	2	1	Design tests which measure accomplishments of trainees.	5	4	3	2	1
5	4	3	2	1	Conduct and evaluate research on training and development.	5	4	3	2	1

Now use the column at the right to show your preferences for the twelve tasks:

> *5 indicates that you enjoy doing the task enough to look forward to it;*
> *4 shows that you rather enjoy doing the task.*
> *3 indicates that you don't care much one way or the other.*
> *2 shows that you would just as soon not do the task.*
> *1 indicates that you will avoid the task when possible.*

Reprinted with permission of the editors, *The Training and Development Sourcebook.* © 1984

HRD Press, 22 Amherst Rd., Amherst, MA 01002. 1-800-822-2801

DESIGN Of Needs Survey

Design your approach to surveying needs by using the written material the client (or others) gives you, along with data collected in your brief interviews with the client and a few other names in the *CONTACT* session.

- Gather historical paper data. Make copies of your own that you can mark or cut up.
  Good sources:
  > Organization plans and objectives
  > Performance appraisals
  > Training programs
  > Audit reports
  > Exit interviews
  > Attitude surveys
  > Industrial engineering
  > Employment figures
  > Job descriptions

- Common survey methods: Questionnaire, interview, test, observation

- Survey design considerations:

If MORE ...		*IF LESS ...*
Open-ended, interviews	Collection Time Available	Closed ended, checklist
Less structured approach	Experience of Data Collectors	More structured approach
Mail instrument	Geographic Spread	Face-to-Face
More structure	Participants	Less structure
Less notes	Confidentiality	More notes
More coding	Amount of Data	Less coding

- Simpler methods are easier for you to use and for the client to understand

- Focus the questions in the survey on individual, group, or organization performance problems or opportunities—not on training needed.

Questions to Ask in Determining Training Needs

When you encounter symptoms of training needs, you need a repertoire of questions to use in validating the training need. Here are some samples for you to rate as USEFUL or NOT USEFUL, indicating the degree of usefulness by a check in the proper place.

Useful				Not Useful		
Very	**Quite**	**Somewhat**		**Trivial**	**Ambiguous**	**Dangerous**
_____	_____	_____	1. What are your training needs?	_____	_____	_____
_____	_____	_____	2. What are the training needs of your employees?	_____	_____	_____
_____	_____	_____	3. What are your big problems?	_____	_____	_____
_____	_____	_____	4. What are the big "people problems" in your span of control?	_____	_____	_____
_____	_____	_____	5. Do your employees have attitudes that need changing?	_____	_____	_____
_____	_____	_____	6. What visible behaviors do these attitudes produce?	_____	_____	_____
_____	_____	_____	7. Can you be more specific?	_____	_____	_____
_____	_____	_____	8. What are they doing that they shouldn't do?	_____	_____	_____
_____	_____	_____	9. What aren't they doing that they should do?	_____	_____	_____
_____	_____	_____	10. What do you feel you need to know in order to do your job better?	_____	_____	_____
_____	_____	_____	11. In what skills do you need practice so you can perform better?	_____	_____	_____
_____	_____	_____	12. (Add your own! On the rest of this page, and the reverse side, jot down helpful/fatal questions from your own experience. We'll have time to discuss these.)	_____	_____	_____

While You Are Collecting Needs ...

- Ask questions about what organization and individual performance is needed—that's what people know about, have expertise in. Respect and listen to their thoughts on performance.

- Don't ask questions about what training is needed. Training questions can imply they have the training expertise to respond and that you are going to act on their training suggestions.

- While collecting data, just collect; don't analyze. Keep the separation clean.

- Collect and code data on cards (one data bit per card) for easy sorting.

- Collect only as much data as you can analyze.

- Help others understand the "how" (process) and "why" (objective) of what you are doing with them.

- Be as open with them as you expect them to be with you.

Needs Survey Checklist

Directions for use: Read this list over carefully. Circle the "Yes" for areas you want training in. Circle the question mark if you are uncertain, or "No" if you need no improvement on your own job or for promotion to a better job.

1. How to train people quickly and easily. Yes ? No
2. How to lead or direct others .... Yes ? No
3. How to plan .... Yes ? No
4. How to control .... Yes ? No
5. How to organize .... Yes ? No
6. How to interpret and apply company policies and procedures .... Yes ? No
7. How to get out more work—motivate people .... Yes ? No
8. How to discipline workers.................... Yes ? No
9. How to improve job methods .... Yes ? No
10. How to do research work..................... Yes ? No
11. How to learn a new job .... Yes ? No
12. How to understand yourself and others—sensitivity............................... Yes ? No
13. How to break down a job into elements... Yes ? No
14. How to work out new ideas.................. Yes ? No
15. How to develop your own manual skill... Yes ? No
16. How to keep machines in working condition... Yes ? No
17. How to keep things in order .... Yes ? No
18. How to evaluate and rate employee's performance...................................... Yes ? No
19. How to reduce waste (time, materials, supplies) .... Yes ? No
20. How to improve your performance on the job... Yes ? No
21. How to improve the morale of your unit... Yes ? No
22. How to sell ideas to a superior .... Yes ? No
23. How to manage the boss....................... Yes ? No
24. How to delegate authority..................... Yes ? No
25. How to help people responsible for results.. Yes ? No
26. How to get people to work together— cooperate... Yes ? No
27. How to be diplomatic—tactful .... Yes ? No
28. How to improve your written and oral expression .... Yes ? No
29. How to recognize details that count...... Yes ? No
30. How to read blueprints and drawings ... Yes ? No
31. How to read charts and tables............... Yes ? No
32. How to improve reading and speaking ability.. Yes ? No
33. How to improve your memory .... Yes ? No
34. How to recognize causes of fatigue ...... Yes ? No
35. How to reduce disagreeable factors on jobs.. Yes ? No
36. How to sell safety to your workers— prevent accidents .... Yes ? No
37. How to work more comfortably .... Yes ? No
38. How to avoid tensions—conflicts......... Yes ? No
39. How to conduct conferences and staff meetings.. Yes ? No
40. How to communicate—upwards, downwards, etc. .... Yes ? No
41. How to interview others....................... Yes ? No
42. How to apply the principles of management... Yes ? No
43. How to make staff studies and do staff work.. Yes ? No
44. How to make or write reports .... Yes ? No
45. How to supervise women employees.... Yes ? No
46. How to supervise minority employees.. Yes ? No

Reprinted with permission of the editors, *The Training and Development Sourcebook.* © 1984

HRD Press, 22 Amherst Rd., Amherst, MA 01002. 1-800-822-2801

Course Evaluation

Course _____ Date _____

		YES	NO

1. Course Objectives
   a. Were they fully explained? ☐ ☐
   b. Were they reviewed during the program? ☐ ☐
   c. Were they reviewed at the conclusion of the program? ☐ ☐
   COMMENTS:

2. a. Do you feel there was sufficient time and opportunity for questions and discussion by ☐ ☐
   the group?
   b. Were the questions raised dealt with, either by the instructor(s) or the group? ☐ ☐
   COMMENTS:

3. What benefits do you feel you got from this session?
   ☐ New knowledge that is pertinent.
   ☐ Specific approaches, skills or techniques that I can apply on the job.
   ☐ Change of attitude that will help me in my job.
   Other:

4. What do you feel are the major strengths of this course?

5. What is your evaluation of the student materials?

6. For items *a* through *f*, mark your response   4   Strongly Agree   2   Disagree
   using these codes.   3   Agree   1   Strongly Disagree

   _____ a. The course content has been valuable for   _____ d. Class time was well used.
        my professional or personal development.   _____ e. The amount of coursework required
   _____ b. The course was well organized.   was appropriate.
   _____ c. The objectives set at the beginning of the   _____ f. The instruction in this class was excellent
        course were met.

7. Would you recommend this course to your associates? If no, why not?

8. What significant changes can you recommend for improving future programs?

9. Please add any other comments you would like to make about any aspect of the course (instructor(s), materials, topics covered, etc.).

10. Please indicate your overall evaluation of this course.

Excellent					*Good*					*Satisfactory*					*Unsatisfactory*			
20	19	18	17	16	15	14	13	12	11	10	9	8	7	6	5	4	3	2	1

Optional: Agency _____ Name _____

Classroom Observation Guide

A classroom observation guide must be designed to collect information about the extent to which training objectives are being met, and identify those factors in the instructional process which appear to impede or facilitate trainees' attainment of the objectives. Our sample classroom observation guide (over) has these main parts:

1. *Training objectives.* These provide a frame of reference within which the observer will base his judgments about the extent of objective attainment.

2. *Assessment.* Here the observer indicates the extent to which the objectives appear to have been attained by the trainees.

3. *Checks on attainment.* Here the observer is required to identify and judge the effectiveness of the checks made by the instructor during the session to monitor the extent to which training objectives are being attained.

4. *Factors influencing objective attainment.* The observer is required to add specificity to the general assessment which he made in 2 above.

The classroom observation approach differs from other methods in that the emphasis is on an individual *observing* the training situation and *making informed judgments* about the extent to which the objectives are being met. If the observation is to contribute significantly to the evaluation effort, the observer should have a sound background in the subject matter of the session he is monitoring, a precise knowledge of its training objectives, and an awareness of how this session ties into the entire instructional program.

The observer's presence during class should not be conspicuous. Therefore, the sample observation form has been designed to allow the observer to check the appropriate blocks during the session and fill in the required explanation later.

After the session, the observer should discuss with the instructor those factors which were believed to have facilitated or impeded the attainment of training objectives. Where appropriate, the oral critique should be followed by a written report in which effective and ineffective aspects previously discussed are noted along with recommendations for improvement. Such reports assume additional importance after the trainee performance data has been obtained, since performance data only indicates *what* has occurred while the observation reports along with opinion surveys can be used to explain *why* the trainees did or did not meet the objectives.

Classroom Observation Guide

Course _____ Session_____

Time_____ Date_____ Instructor_____

1. Training objectives:_____
_____
_____
_____

2. **Assessment:** To what extent did training objectives appear to be attained? (Adverse factors should be explained in item 4 below.)
   a. ☐ Fully. (Minor deficiencies, if any.)
   b. ☐ Partially. (Some factors preventing full achievement.)
   c. ☐ Hardly at all.

Continued. . .

3. **Checks on attainment:** What steps did the instructor take to assure himself that training objectives were being attained?_____

_____

_____

How effective were they?_____

_____

4. **Factors influencing objective attainment**: Factors that had an adverse effect on training objective attainment as indicated in 2 above. (Check any such factors and explain on the back of this sheet.)

Factor	Check	Factor	Check
A. Introduction to training session	_____	I. Instructor's ability to direct discussion	_____
B. Content	_____	J. Appropriateness of material to group	_____
C. Clarity of explanations	_____	K. Time/material relationship	_____
D. Instructor's apparent knowledge of subject	_____	L. Individual trainee involvement	_____
E. Subject matter organization	_____	M. Instructional methods used	_____
F. Selection and use of training aids	_____	N. Reference materials	_____
G. Instructor's manner (tact, etc.)	_____	O. Classroom facilities	_____
H. Instructor's ability to maintain trainees' interest	_____	P. Tests and practical exercises	_____
		Q. Other (specify)	_____

_____

(Observer's Name)

Workshop in Training Course Design

"This Is How It All Was"   Participant Opinion

1. Referring to your list of terminal objectives, please respond to the questions below by checking the appropriate blocks. Do elaborate or explain your opinion wherever you think it helpful to our assessment and improvement of the course.

(1) Major training objectives (refer to objective statements)	(2) As far as you are concerned, was this objective achieved?			(3) If the objective was not at all, or only partially achieved, what factors were responsible? (Please check and explain below)									(4) Do you believe that this objective was related to the requirements of your job?			(5) Do you believe the benefits derived from pursuing this objective were worth the time and effort?		
	Definitely	To some extent	Not at all	The instructor	Lesson content	Instructional methods	Instructional level	Time allocation	Test & practical exercises	Training aids	Classroom facilities	Other	Definitely	To some extent	Not at all	Definitely	To some extent	Not at all
No. I																		
No. II																		
No. III																		

Objective No.	Explanations:

Modeled on materials developed by and for the U.S. Civil Service Commission.

Group Work Evaluation Form

Please score the following questions along the scales provided: (1) represents the lowest rating and (9), the highest.

1. *Membership:* How much did you feel that you were a fully-functioning and accepted member of your group?

LOW   1   2   3   4   5   6   7   8   9   HIGH

2. *Goals:* How well-defined and clear was the purpose of your group?

LOW   1   2   3   4   5   6   7   8   9   HIGH

3. *Task:* How well did your group contribute to your understanding of the personal reactions and particular issues you presented to the group?

LOW   1   2   3   4   5   6   7   8   9   HIGH

4. *Process:* How much did you learn about group processes and how groups function?

LOW   1   2   3   4   5   6   7   8   9   HIGH

5. *Support:* How helped and/or supported did you feel in your group?

LOW   1   2   3   4   5   6   7   8   9   HIGH

6. *Value:* How valuable were your group sessions in terms of your course objectives?

LOW   1   2   3   4   5   6   7   8   9   HIGH

7. Additional Comments and Suggestions:

Name_____:

(optional)

Date:_____

CHAPTER VI

Performance Appraisal Questionnaires

Questionnaire 1

ATTITUDES TOWARD PERFORMANCE APPRAISAL

Indicate your opinion of the performance appraisal system you have been using by completing each of the following statement. Circle your responses.

The Performance Appraisal System...	Agree	Not Sure	Disagree
1....measures all relevant dimensions of performance.	A	?	D
2....is objective.	A	?	D
3....is accepted as legitimate and important by the organization.	A	?	D
4....is constructive and enhances employee development.	A	?	D
5....is an integral part of managing.	A	?	D
6....is useful in the planning and job staffing processes.	A	?	D
7....is uniform across the organization.	A	?	D
8....is clearly understood by those who use it.	A	?	D
9....is useful in performing supervisory responsibilities.	A	?	D
10....is regularly used as a basis for various personnel actions.	A	?	D

Reprinted with permission of the editors, *The Performance Appraisal Sourcebook.* © 1983

HRD Press, 22 Amherst Rd., Amherst, MA 01002. 1-800-822-2801

Questionnaire 2
A SAMPLE SELF-APPRAISAL FORM

The questions below are designed to stimulate your thinking, and to help you prepare for the appraisal session and get maximum benefit from it. Think about your own personal performance, progress, and plans for future improvement. Appraise yourself. When finished, this form may be given to your superior or retained by you.

1. What do I consider to be the important abilities which my job requires?

2. What are some aspects of my job that I like best? That I like least?

3. What are the ways in which my superiors can help me to do my job better?

4. In what aspects of my job do I feel I need more experience and training?

5. What are my major accomplishments for the past year?

6. What have I done for my personal and/or professional development?

7. Are there any changes I would like to see made in my job which would improve my effectiveness?

8. Are all of my capabilities being utilized in my present position? If not, how can they be better utilized?

9. What are specific things I need to do in the next year for my own development?

10. In what ways would my present position better prepare me for assuming more responsibility?

11. What are my long range plans? What type of work do I see myself doing five years from now? How am I preparing myself for this work?

Reprinted with permission of the editors, *The Performance Appraisal Sourcebook.* © 1983
HRD Press, 22 Amherst Rd., Amherst, MA 01002. 1-800-822-2801

OBSERVER WORKSHEET FOR MANAGING PERFORMANCE PROBLEMS

1. Clarification of purpose

a. Was the purpose of the discussion made clear in the beginning?

b. Was the problem to be addressed described in specific terms?

2. Preview of topics

After the purpose of the discussion is clarified, the person being interviewed will usually be asking him/herself "What kind of information does he/she want?" Rather than let him/her guess as the discussion goes from question to question, it is best to lay out the topics initially and suggest a way of talking about them.

a. Was it clear what topics were to be discussed?

b. Did the participants have a chance to talk about how to conduct the discussion?

3. Motivation of interviewee

The person interviewed must be involved. His/her views are important and a commitment to the solution is critical. A good way to assess how involved the interviewer gets the other person is to consider the types of questions that were asked and how much listening the interviewer did.

a. Did the interviewer ask relevant questions? Did the interviewer spend too much time trying to give answers and tell the other person what to do?

Continued. . .

b. Did the interviewer listen? Did the interviewer spend too much time talking?

c. Did the person interviewed have a chance to participate in defining the problem?

4. Body of the discussion

a. Did the participants jump too quickly to try to solve the problem before it was accurately described?

b. Did the participants agree on what the problem was?

5. Summary

a. Did the participants reach a conclusion?

b. Did both participants leave with a clear understanding of what each was going to do (action plans) to solve the problem?

c. Did they set times for completing the actions and getting back together? Were feedback mechanisms put in place?

Reprinted with permission of the editors, *The Performance Appraisal Sourcebook.* © 1983
HRD Press, 22 Amherst Rd., Amherst, MA 01002. 1-800-822-2801

CHAPTER VII

Performance Management Questionnaires and Assessments

A Self-Assessment of Your Performance Management Practices

Answer each question below as honestly as you can. The exercise is for your use only. Scoring instructions follow.

1. You communicate high personal standards informally—in conversation, personal appearance, etc.

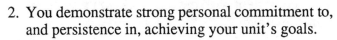

5	4	3	2	1

Very descriptive of my practices   Not at all descriptive of my practices

2. You demonstrate strong personal commitment to, and persistence in, achieving your unit's goals.

5	4	3	2	1

Very descriptive of my practices   Not at all descriptive of my practices

3. Your staff members have a chance to influence the performance goals and standards that are set for their jobs.

5	4	3	2	1

Very descriptive of my practices   Not at all descriptive of my practices

4. You establish clear, specific performance goals and standards for staff members' jobs.

5	4	3	2	1

Very descriptive of my practices   Not at all descriptive of my practices

5. You help staff members understand how their jobs contribute to the overall effectiveness of the work group.

5	4	3	2	1

Very descriptive of my practices   Not at all descriptive of my practices

6. You ask staff members to participate in setting deadlines for the achievement of their goals.

5	4	3	2	1

Very descriptive of my practices   Not at all descriptive of my practices

7. You ask staff members to participate in deciding on which of their goals are most important.

5	4	3	2	1

Very descriptive of my practices   Not at all descriptive of my practices

8. Your staff members have a clear understanding of their duties and responsibilities.

5	4	3	2	1

Very descriptive of my practices   Not at all descriptive of my practices

9. You build warm, friendly relationships with the people in your work group, rather than remaining cool and impersonal.

5	4	3	2	1

Very descriptive of my practices   Not at all descriptive of my practices

10. You try to make the best use of staff members' skills and abilities when making assignments.

5	4	3	2	1

Very descriptive of my practices   Not at all descriptive of my practices

11. If you feel your staff members are right, you will definitely go to bat for them with your superiors.

5	4	3	2	1

Very descriptive of my practices   Not at all descriptive of my practices

12. You provide help, training, and guidance so that staff members can improve their performance.

5	4	3	2	1

Very descriptive of my practices   Not at all descriptive of my practices

Continued. . .

13. You pay close attention to what staff members are saying when they talk to you.

5	4	3	2	1

Very descriptive of my practices — Not at all descriptive of my practices

14. Your staff members can be completely open in telling you about their mistakes.

5	4	3	2	1

Very descriptive of my practices — Not at all descriptive of my practices

15. Your staff members can get a clear-cut decision from you when they need one.

5	4	3	2	1

Very descriptive of my practices — Not at all descriptive of my practices

16. You prepare staff members to fill in for each other when key people are absent or unavailable.

5	4	3	2	1

Very descriptive of my practices — Not at all descriptive of my practices

17. You communicate your views honestly and directly during discussions of staff members' performance.

5	4	3	2	1

Very descriptive of my practices — Not at all descriptive of my practices

18. You consider relevant information when appraising staff members' performance.

5	4	3	2	1

Very descriptive of my practices — Not at all descriptive of my practices

19. You work with staff members to reach mutual agreement on their performance appraisals.

5	4	3	2	1

Very descriptive of my practices — Not at all descriptive of my practices

20. You help staff members develop specific plans to improve their performance.

5	4	3	2	1

Very descriptive of my practices — Not at all descriptive of my practices

21. You work with staff members to determine their realistic short-term career objectives.

5	4	3	2	1

Very descriptive of my practices — Not at all descriptive of my practices

22. You give staff members feedback on how they are doing on their jobs.

5	4	3	2	1

Very descriptive of my practices — Not at all descriptive of my practices

23. Your staff members' written performance appraisals are consistent with the feedback you give them informally.

5	4	3	2	1

Very descriptive of my practices — Not at all descriptive of my practices

24. You explain to staff members the factors used in judging their performance.

5	4	3	2	1

Very descriptive of my practices — Not at all descriptive of my practices

25. You sit down regularly with staff members to review their overall performance.

5	4	3	2	1

Very descriptive of my practices — Not at all descriptive of my practices

26. You use recognition and praise (aside from pay) to reward excellent performance.

5	4	3	2	1

Very descriptive of my practices — Not at all descriptive of my practices

27. You are more likely to recognize staff members for good performance than to criticze them for performance problems.

5	4	3	2	1

Very descriptive of my practices — Not at all descriptive of my practices

Continued. . .

28. You provide staff members with the information they need regarding pay and other compensation policies.

5	4	3	2	1

Very descriptive
of my practices

Not at all descriptive
of my practices

29. You make every effort to be fair with staff members regarding their pay.

5	4	3	2	1

Very descriptive
of my practices

Not at all descriptive
of my practices

30. You notice and show appreciation when staff members have put in extra time and effort.

5	4	3	2	1

Very descriptive
of my practices

Not at all descriptive
of my practices

31. You relate rewards (salary increases, recognition, promotions) to excellence of job performance rather than to other factors such as personal relationships.

5	4	3	2	1

Very descriptive
of my practices

Not at all descriptive
of my practices

32. The work-group meetings you conduct serve to increase trust and mutual respect among work-group members.

5	4	3	2	1

Very descriptive
of my practices

Not at all descriptive
of my practices

33. You make sure there is a frank and open exchange of ideas in work-group meetings.

5	4	3	2	1

Very descriptive
of my practices

Not at all descriptive
of my practices

34. You periodically try to get a feel for work-group morale.

5	4	3	2	1

Very descriptive
of my practices

Not at all descriptive
of my practices

35. You emphasize cooperation as opposed to competitiveness among members of your work group.

5	4	3	2	1

Very descriptive
of my practices

Not at all descriptive
of my practices

36. When conflicts arise in your work group, you make an effort to work them out with the individuals involved.

5	4	3	2	1

Very descriptive
of my practices

Not at all descriptive
of my practices

37. You establish departmental or work-group goals.

5	4	3	2	1

Very descriptive
of my practices

Not at all descriptive
of my practices

38. The work-group meetings you hold are well-organized and thought out.

5	4	3	2	1

Very descriptive
of my practices

Not at all descriptive
of my practices

39. Your staff members have a clear understanding of what was decided at the end of work-group meetings you hold.

5	4	3	2	1

Very descriptive
of my practices

Not at all descriptive
of my practices

HRD Press, 22 Amherst Rd., Amherst, MA 01002. 1-800-822-2801

Scoring the Self-Assessment Questionnaire

Instructions: Give yourself 5 points for each question for which you checked the line above the "5" on the scale, 4 points for each question for which you checked the line above the "4" on the scale, etc. There are five separate scores, derived from summing your scores in each column.

1 Setting and Communicating Performance Expectations	2 On-going Coaching, Counseling, Feedback, Management	3 Appraising and Receiving	4 Recognizing and Rewarding	5 Managing Group Performance
1. _____	9. _____	17. _____	26. _____	32. _____
2. _____	10. _____	18. _____	27. _____	33. _____
3. _____	11. _____	19. _____	28. _____	34. _____
4. _____	12.. _____	20. _____	29. _____	35. _____
5. _____	13. _____	21. _____	30. _____	36. _____
6. _____	14. _____	22. _____	31. _____	37. _____
7. _____	15. _____	23. _____		38. _____
8. _____	16. _____	24. _____		39. _____
		25. _____		
TOTAL:_____ (40 possible)	TOTAL:_____ (40 possible)	TOTAL:_____ (45 possible)	TOTAL:_____ (30 possible)	TOTAL:_____ (40 possible)

YOUR PM STRENGTHS:_____

_____

_____

_____

YOUR PM WEAKNESSES: _____

_____

_____

_____

Reprinted with permission of the editors, *The Performance Management Sourcebook.* © 1987

HRD Press, 22 Amherst Rd., Amherst, MA 01002. 1-800-822-2801

Performance Management Practices Questionnaire

Instructions: First, for each of the following statements, please indicate how often an excellent manager should do each of the statements. Please place a check (✔) to indicate this level of frequency in the appropriate column.

Second, please think of your own behavior as a supervisor/manager. then, indicate how frequently you do each of the following by placing an "X" in the appropriate column. Please be certain that you have assessed your observations of your own behavior and not what you intended to do.

	Never	Seldom	Occasionally	Frequently	Always
A. Strategic Performance Planning Linkage					
1. Insure that goals of your strategic work unit's (SWU) goals are consistent with strategic company goals.					
2. Insure that your employees are aware of operating company goals.					
3. Insure that employees are aware of Corporate goals.					
4. Establish clear, specific work unit goals and standards linked with operating company goals.					
5. Help staff members understand how their jobs contribute to company goals and corporate goals.					
B. Gaining Employee Commitment					
6. Communicate higher personal standards informally—in conversation, personal example, etc.					
7. Demonstrate strong personal commitment to, and persistence in, achieving your unit's goals.					
8. Ask staff members to participate in setting deadlines for the achievement of their goals.					
9. Build warm, friendly relationships with the people in your work group, rather than remaining cool and impersonal.					
10. Conduct work unit meetings to increase trust and mutual respect among members.					
11. Attempt to get a "feel" for work unit morale.					
12. Emphasize cooperation as opposed to competitiveness among members of your work group.					
13. When conflicts arise, make an effort to work them out with the individuals involved.					
C. Setting Work Unit Goals					
14. Establish clear-cut goals for every direct report.					
15. Develop measures to evaluate programs toward work unit goals.					

Continued. . .

	Never	Seldom	Occasionally	Frequently	Always
16. Develop an awareness of the methods of measurement for your work unit goals.					
17. Make certain there is a frank and open exchange of ideas in work-group meetings.					
18. Hold meetings that are well-organized and well thought out.					
19. Insure staff members have a clear understanding of what was decided at the end of work-group meetings you conduct.					
20. Ask if staff members have a clear understanding of their duties and responsibilities.					
21. Provide staff members with clear-cut decisions when needed.					

D. Negotiating Individual Performance Goals and Standards

	Never	Seldom	Occasionally	Frequently	Always
22. Give staff members a chance to influence the performance goals and standards that are set for their jobs.					
23. Ask staff members to participate in deciding on which goals are most important.					
24. Make the best use of staff members' skills and abilities when making assignments.					
25. Explain to staff members the factors used in evaluating their performance.					
26. Set clear-cut, individual assignment measures.					
27. Set clear-cut work standards (measures of behaviors and outcomes).					

E. Observing Employee Performance

	Never	Seldom	Occasionally	Frequently	Always
28. Pay close attention to what staff members are saying when they talk to you.					
29. Communicate your views honestly and directly during discussions of staff members' performance.					

F. Documenting Employee Performance

	Never	Seldom	Occasionally	Frequently	Always
30. Consider all relevant information when appraising staff members' performance.					
31. Make every effort to gather information to enable you to accurately evaluate an employee's performance.					

G. Giving Feedback and Coaching Employees

	Never	Seldom	Occasionally	Frequently	Always
32. Provide training with specific behavioral feedback to enable employees to improve their performance.					
33. Provide a climate whereby staff members can be completely open in telling you about their mistakes.					

Continued. . .

	Never	Seldom	Occasionally	Frequently	Always
34. Prepare employees to fill in for each other when key people are absent or unavailable.					
35. Help employees develop specific plans to improve their performance.					
36. Work with employees to determine their realistic short-term career objectives.					
37. Give employees verbal feedback on how well they are doing on their jobs.					
38. Give staff members written feedback on how well they are doing on their jobs.					
39. Recognize and praise excellent performance.					
40. Recognize staff members for good performance more often than criticizing for performance problems.					
41. Notice and show appreciation when staff members have put in extra time and effort.					
42. Go to bat for your employees with your superiors when your employees are "right."					

H. Conducting Formal Performance Reviews

	Never	Seldom	Occasionally	Frequently	Always
43. Work with employees to reach mutual agreement on performance appraisals.					
44. Give employees written performance appraisals consistent with the feedback you have given them informally during the performance period.					
45. Sit down frequently with employees to review their overall performance.					
46. Provide employees with the information they need regarding pay and other compensation policies.					

I. Rewarding Performance with Pay

	Never	Seldom	Occasionally	Frequently	Always
47. Make every effort to be fair with staff members regarding their pay.					
48. Relate rewards (salary increases, recognition, promotions) to excellence in job performance rather than to other factors such as personal relationships.					

Reprinted with permission of the editors, *The Performance Management Sourcebook.* © 1987

HRD Press, 22 Amherst Rd., Amherst, MA 01002. 1-800-822-2801

Optional Questions

Now that you have completed this questionnaire, you may wish to verify your views of your managerial behaviors with the observations of those who report to you.

> All of the following questions are prefixed with the statement **"Does your manager?"**:

Ask you to develop goals and standards of evaluation before meeting with you to discuss these

Meet with you to renegotiate goals and standards when work assignments or priorities change

Use behavior-based language in documentary performance

Avoid using assumptions about employee know-how (vs. employee behavior) in evaluating employee performance

Avoid using adjectives and conclusions about behavior as opposed to behavior in documentary performance

Record all feedback (both positive and negative) given to employees

Know as immediately as possible how you are doing both positively and negatively

Give praise immediately when you reach performance standards

Give a reprimand when you do not meet performance expectations

Except in extreme instances, reprimand in private

Make certain that all documented observations of behavior are fed back to employees

Evaluating/Rating Employee Performance

Attempt to minimize rating errors (e.g., Halo, contrast, leniency/strictness, control tendency, etc.)

Attempt to maximize rating accuracy

Use only task-related behaviors and outcomes to evaluate performance

Base evaluations on documentation of behavior during the performance evaluation period

Avoid having ratings influenced by performance outside the specific rating period

Check with other relevant observers of employee's performance for documented observations

Conducting Formal Performance Reviews

Provide at least one to four hours for each employee's annual review

See to it that you are not interrupted during the formal review (i.e., no phone calls, interruptions by secretaries, etc.)

Make eye contact throughout the review

Smile at appropriate times during the review

Use the employee's first name throughout the review

Let the employee know that you are available as a resource to help them improve performance

Rewarding Performance with Pay

Develop a clear, linear relationship between performance and pay

 HRD Press, 22 Amherst Rd., Amherst, MA 01002. 1-800-822-2801

Profile of Your Actual/Ideal Performance Management Program

Think about the history of Performance Management in your organization. Mark with an "A" on the scales (1-7) below where you ACTUALLY are, and mark with an "I" where IDEALLY you would like the organization to be within three years (1 not at all—7 a great deal).

I. MY ORGANIZATION...

A. 1_____2_____3_____4_____5_____6_____ ☐ 7
Encourages managers to involve employees in key organization decisions.

B. 1_____2_____3_____4_____5_____6_____ ☐ 7
Regularly communicates senior management's "vision" and objectives throughout the organization.

C. 1_____2_____3_____4_____5_____6_____ ☐ 7
Expects every employee/manager to contribute in achieving the organization's most important objectives.

D. 1_____2_____3_____4_____5_____6_____ ☐ 7
Is an outstanding place to work.

II. IN MY ORGANIZATION, THE PERFORMANCE MANAGEMENT SYSTEM...

A. 1_____2_____3_____4_____5_____6_____ ☐ 7
Is an ongoing management process, with meaningful communication which is linked to the critical plans and objectives of the organization.

B. 1_____2_____3_____4_____5_____6_____ ☐ 7
Was developed with input from employees/managers throughout the organization.

C. 1_____2_____3_____4_____5_____6_____ ☐ 7
Is "owned" by every manager/employee and seen as one of their most critical responsibilities.

D. 1_____2_____3_____4_____5_____6_____ ☐ 7
Includes extensive orientation and training for everyone impacted.

E. 1_____2_____3_____4_____5_____6_____ ☐ 7
Is viewed as a valuable tool for managing how work gets done and how well each individual is performing.

F. 1_____2_____3_____4_____5_____6_____ ☐ 7
Is legally defensible.

III. IN MY ORGANIZATION...

A. 1_____2_____3_____4_____5_____6_____ ☐ 7
Senior management is INVOLVED/COMMITTED to the successful implementation of our performance management system.

B. 1_____2_____3_____4_____5_____6_____ ☐ 7
Middle management is INVOLVED/COMMITTED to the successful implementation of our performance management system.

C. 1_____2_____3_____4_____5_____6_____ ☐ 7
Supervisors are INVOLVED/COMMITTED to the successful implementation of our performance management system.

Continued. . .

D. 1————2————3————4————5————6———— ☐ 7
Employees are INVOLVED/COMMITTED to the successful implementation of our performance management system.

E. 1————2————3————4————5————6———— ☐ 7
There is a direct link between "strategic/business planning" and the performance management system.

F. 1————2————3————4————5————6———— ☐ 7
The performance management system is used to integrate other key systems (i.e., quality improvement, productivity improvement, succession planning, etc.).

G. 1————2————3————4————5————6———— ☐ 7
Appraisal results are used for promotion decisions.

H. 1————2————3————4————5————6———— ☐ 7
Appraisal results are used for compensation decisions.

I. 1————2————3————4————5————6———— ☐ 7
Appraisal results are used to determine training needs.

IV. THE TRAINING PROVIDED IN SUPPORT OF OUR PERFORMANCE MANAGEMENT SYSTEM...

A. 1————2————3————4————5————6———— ☐ 7
Teaches how to define a job so that it accurately reflects the work to be done.

B. 1————2————3————4————5————6———— ☐ 7
Teaches how to develop qualitative and quantitative definitions of successful performance (standards).

C. 1————2————3————4————5————6———— ☐ 7
Teaches how to keep track of one's performance relative to the standards which are in place.

D. 1————2————3————4————5————6———— ☐ 7
Teaches how to provide positive feedback for a job well done.

E. 1————2————3————4————5————6———— ☐ 7
Teaches how to provide corrective feedback for those areas needing improvement.

F. 1————2————3————4————5————6———— ☐ 7
Teaches how to use appraisal forms and follow appraisal procedures.

G. 1————2————3————4————5————6———— ☐ 7
Teaches managers how to solve performance problems.

H. 1————2————3————4————5————6———— ☐ 7
Teaches how to use this system as an employee development tool.

I. 1————2————3————4————5————6———— ☐ 7
Gives ample opportunity for managers/supervisors to practice their skills before returning to the job.

J. 1————2————3————4————5————6———— ☐ 7
Includes ways to measure how effectively skills are being used back on the job.

HRD Press, 22 Amherst Rd., Amherst, MA 01002. 1-800-822-2801

Performance Management Workshop Evaluation: Short Form

1. The workshop *content* was appropriate and useful.

__5__	__4__	__3__	__2__	__1__
Extremely Appropriate				Not At All Appropriate

2. The workshop teaching and training *methods* were appropriate and effective.

__5__	__4__	__3__	__2__	__1__
Extremely Appropriate				Not At All Appropriate

3. The workshop *materials* provided for me were appropriate and useful.

__5__	__4__	__3__	__2__	__1__
Extremely Appropriate				Not At All Appropriate

4. The workshop *instructor(s)* was (were) effective.

__5__	__4__	__3__	__2__	__1__
Extremely Appropriate				Not At All Appropriate

5. The workshop provided *useful and practical* ideas and suggestions I can apply in my organization.

__5__	__4__	__3__	__2__	__1__
Extremely Appropriate				Not At All Appropriate

6. I *know and understand more* about performance management than I did before the workshop.

__5__	__4__	__3__	__2__	__1__
Extremely Appropriate				Not At All Appropriate

7. *Overall,* the workshop was a beneficial and useful experience.

__5__	__4__	__3__	__2__	__1__
Extremely Appropriate				Not At All Appropriate

8. What did you find *most effective*, useful, appropriate?

_____

_____

_____

_____

9. What did you find *least effective*, useful, appropriate?

_____

_____

_____

_____

10. Would you *recommend* this workshop to others interested in the design, implementation, and evaluation of performance management systems?

_____ YES   _____ NO

Why or why not?_____

_____

_____

_____

HRD Press, 22 Amherst Rd., Amherst, MA 01002. 1-800-822-2801

Case Study

State Patrol

In the Midwest, one of the larger state patrols was faced with the imminent retirement of many of its higher level officers. The State's Governor had begun to address this issue by the appointment of a relatively young captain to the role of chief of the state patrol. The new chief was about to make eleven promotions to major and thirty-one promotions to captain and forty-six promotions to lieutenant within the next two years, all created by retirements and forecasted attrition.

Historically the organization had been using assessment centers to select its next managers. The chief was supportive of this idea since he himself had been selected through the assessment center process, through which he had skipped the rank of Major upon his promotion to Chief. However, he was also concerned by the time and cost of assessment centers and enamored by the prospects that the subordinates of each of his "managers" might have as good as if not better data on their manager's performance on many of the same dimensions examined in the assessment center. Further, he had always questioned the relationship between the assessment center and specific performance dimensions found in the work planning and review performance appraisal system which the patrol had been using for some years. He liked the work planning and review system because he felt it gave him enough flexibility to accomplish the strategic change he was asked to bring about within the patrol as requested by the Governor. He also wondered if subordinate data might not be more accurate data than provided in the assessment center was a "simulation," and not an actual work sample.

Henry Hudson was the Patrol's new personnel manager, and a recent graduate of a local university with an MBA in Human Resources. He was summoned by the chief and asked to design a "bottom up" performance appraisal system to assess each manager by their subordinates as part of a broader survey of organizational performance. He was also asked to determine the costs and accuracy of predicting officer's performance after promotion positions with subordinate assessment as well as with historic performance appraisals. The chief was adamant that the dimensions assessed by subordinate appraisals be the same as those used by the assessment center to predict managerial success.

The chief also asked Henry Hudson to keep careful records of his expenditures in order to definitively compare the costs of "bottoms up" prediction of managerial performance versus assessment centers and/or historic appraisals.

Instructions. You are to assume the role of Henry Hudson and to make specific recommendations for the content and the design of the subordinate appraisal system as well as the procedures by which the subordinate appraisal system would be administered, data collected, and method of data analysis. You are to determine how the success of one technique would be compared to the cost/benefits of alternatives.

Reprinted with permission of the editors, *The Performance Management Sourcebook.* © 1987

HRD Press, 22 Amherst Rd., Amherst, MA 01002. 1-800-822-2801